# Prayer Warriors: Serious Minded Pray-ers

*"The end of all things is at hand; therefore, be of sound judgment and sober [serious] spirit for the purpose of prayer."*
(1 Peter 4:7 NASB)

### Dr. Leroy Jolly

*Priority*ONE
*publications*
Detroit, MI USA

*Prayer Warriors: Serious Minded Pray-ers*
Copyright © 1999, 2005 2nd Edition Leroy Jolly

---

All scripture quotations, unless otherwise indicated, are taken from the New King James Version®. Copyright © 1982 by Thomas Nelson, Inc. Used by permission. All rights reserved.

Scripture quotations marked (NIV) are taken from the New International Version®. NIV®. Copyright ©1973, 1978, 1984 by International Bible Society. Used by permission of Zondervan. All rights reserved.

Scripture quotations marked (AMP) are taken from the Amplified Bible, Copyright © 1954, 1958, 1962, 1964, 1965, 1987 by The Lockman Foundation. Used by permission.

Out of reverence and honor for God's Word, the word Bible is capitalized throughout this work. Also throughout this work the name of satan is not capitalized in order to re-emphasize Christ's victory over him.

An effort has been made to locate sources and obtain permission, where necessary for the quotations used in this book. In the event of any unintentional omission, a modification will gladly be incorporated in future printings.

All rights reserved. No part of this publication may be reproduced, stored in a retrieval system, or transmitted in any form or by any means – electronic, mechanical, photocopy, recording, or any other – except for brief quotations in printed reviews, without the prior permission of the publisher.

*Priority*ONE Publications
P. O. Box 725 • Farmington, MI 48332
(800) 596-4490 Nationwide Toll Free
E-mail: info@p1pubs.com
URL: http://www.p1pubs.com

ISBN: 0-9703634-2-7

*Edited by Patricia Hicks*
*Illustration by Kirby Walter*
*Cover and interior design by PriorityONE Publications*

Printed in the United States of America

# Dedication

I dedicate this "Prayer Book"
to all those who are serious
about prayer and to those
who in their hearts desire to
become faithful "Prayer Warriors."

I especially dedicate this book to
those who attended the college
extension classes I taught and to
those who urged and encouraged me
to write this prayer book.

Also I must mention
Pastor Debra Rau. It was she,
while we were in prayer together,
who received the vision that God had
called me to write this book.

For my wife, Wilma, I give praise!
She is my strongest "Prayer Partner"
and "Prayer Warrior." For years we
have together fought this spiritual warfare
battle through the weapon of prayer!

Every Home for Christ, 700 Club, and
Campus Crusade have all influenced me
to be and remain a "faithful, serious-minded
Prayer Warrior." Amen! and Amen!

"And when He had sent the multitudes
away, He went up on the mountain by
Himself to pray. Now when evening came,
He was alone there" (Matthew 14:23).

# Table of Contents

### PART ONE:
### UNDERSTANDING THE GLORIOUS PRIVILEGE OF PRAYER

Chapter 1: Understanding the Heart of Prayer ................................................... 11
Chapter 2: Understanding the Sphere of Prayer ................................................. 16
Chapter 3: Personal Prayer Evaluation ............................................................... 21
Chapter 4: The Privilege To Pray Motivates Serious-Minded Pray-ers ............. 31
Chapter 5: Seek God Through Prayer First ........................................................ 35
Chapter 6: More Seeking God Through Prayer First ......................................... 43

### PART TWO:
### THE HELPLESSNESS OF JESUS CHRIST GOD'S HOLY SON

Chapter 7: Jesus Christ, a Man of Humility ....................................................... 51
Chapter 8: Jesus Christ, the Man of Helplessness .............................................. 59
Chapter 9: Prayer! — Jesus' Strong Pillar .......................................................... 67
Chapter 10: Jesus' Prayer Life: Our Greatest Example ...................................... 75

### PART THREE:
### THE SPIRITUAL APPLICATION OF PRAYER

Chapter 11: Things Learned ............................................................................... 83
Chapter 12: Confession of Sin a Must ................................................................ 87
Chapter 13: The Spiritual Position for Prayer .................................................... 93
Chapter 14: I Can NOW Pray! HALLELUJAH! ............................................... 105
About the Author ................................................................................................ 117

# Acknowledgment

The birth of this book, *Prayer Warriors: Serious-Minded Pray-ers*, was not born out of an intense desire to write. It certainly wasn't the fact that I possess some spiritual, unique approach to prayer that would make it a dynamic experience. After teaching "Prayer Enrichment Revivals," encouraging the local Church to have "Volunteer Prayer Warriors" who would become the "Prayer Warriors" in the local Church, different people came to me and strongly urged and encouraged me to write a prayer book. Still I was not convinced that I should attempt such a holy, serious, and reverent task.

However, my decision to attempt such an awesome task was radically driven home to me through prayer, not during my praying, but the prayer of a dear lady whom I did not know personally. I met with a group of Christian men and women to pray. At the close of our prayer time after most of the people were gone, I met a lady and two of her friends. We entered into prayer together. After we prayed for several minutes, she entered into prophetic praying. She saw a manuscript with writing on it, a book being written. Through the power of prayer and the inspiration of the Holy Spirit, she said that God had called me to the task of writing a book focusing on prayer. Her prayer and prophecy convicted me and thus I entered into this spiritual challenge.

Needless to say, one of the greatest influences on my life for prayer has been *Every Home for Christ*, which in the 70's was titled, *World Literature Crusade*. While I turned from one TV channel to another one evening, in 1975 or 1976, attempting to find a program worthwhile to watch, Dr. Jack McAlister, who was its founder, was on the television. He was encouraging Christians to commit themselves to 15 minutes per day in prayer and to pray for the needs of the world. I made my call and committed myself to faithful prayer. The influence and serious teaching, through the Holy Spirit, of Dr. McAlister, Dr. Johnny Lee, who replaced Dr. McAlister when he retired, and then Dr. Dick Eastman, who was at that time teaching *Schools of Prayer*, and now the president of *Every Home for Christ*, revolutionized my Christian experience. It led me first into the refreshing waters of prayer, and then later to swim around in the refreshing ocean of teaching "Prayer Enrichment Revivals," which is the height of my joy. I do not possess the literary expertise of these Christian warriors; they don't even know I exist. When I read Dick Eastman's books, *The Hour that Changes the World* and *No Easy Road*, I knew that prayer was to become my personal ministry! Thus, I praise God for *Every Home for Christ* and the birth of this book for whatever spiritual worth it may be to you, the reader!

Leroy Jolly

# Preface

*Frustration! Frustration!* That was my spiritual mindset as I sat down in a Best Western Motel in Abilene, Kansas. In fear and trembling, I reflected on the challenge facing me as I thought about the preface and the introduction to this book I was venturing to write—*Prayer Warriors: Serious-Minded Pray-ers*, I Peter 4:7 being the backdrop.

*"Everything will soon come to an end.*
*So be serious and be sensible enough to pray"* (CEV).

When it comes to the task of penning meaningful, heart-searching words, focusing on the most sacred privilege we Christians have—prayer! Inserting them in a book, to me, has been an impossible task. Even though I have been teaching the meaning, power, and the insights of prayer, using the theme "Becoming Prayer Warriors," which the Lord has given me over a period of years, who am I to attempt such an awesome responsibility? However, the Lord has refused to release me of this burden. In fact, feeling my helplessness and inability, I wrote the following "Prayer Letter" to twelve Prayer Warriors who had been in my prayer sessions and had committed themselves to faithful prayer.

Dear Precious Prayer Warrior,

Proverbs 16: 1-3 TLB states: "We make our [own] plans, but the final outcome [result] is in God's hands. We can always "prove" [argue] that we are right, but is the Lord convinced? Commit your work [purpose] to the Lord, then it will succeed."

The Lord will not release me. He has told me that it is now time! I have argued with Him and have given Him what I have considered to be good, truthful, and solid reasons for not attempting such an assignment. He notified me that they were only excuses, not reasons, and that He did not accept excuses. (A person told me that an excuse is reason with the skin peeled off and stuffed with lies). Thus, it is time the Lord has told me to write my "Prayer Book."

After reading Proverbs 16:1-3, I have committed this

awesome task, this humbling experience, to the Lord. My total purpose is that God's people and the Church will realize that God is the Answer and PRAYER to Him is to be our method of operation! Please pray for me; ask the Lord to give me wisdom and the "How to" in undertaking this tremendous challenge.

Blessed Fellow Prayer Warrior,<br>Bro. Leroy Jolly

Thus, dear readers, through the power of the Holy Spirit and His divine leadership, I said, "Yes, Lord, I am ready to write Your words of prayer!"

# Introduction

At the young age of fourteen, I accepted the Lord as my Savior. Then it was my gracious privilege to lead both my parents to the Lord. During the ages of 15 to 18, I attended every religious function that my Church provided. During these growing years, I led prayer meetings, testified during testimony services, and prayed publicly whenever I was asked. At the age of eighteen I was drafted into the army of World War II. During this totally different experience for me, I at times read my Bible and prayed, not realizing, however, that neither the Word of God nor prayer had really become a daily, serious, prayerful commitment in my spiritual life. I prayed, but I had not grasped the understanding that prayer was and is a glorious privilege extended to God's precious children, that it is to be the *heart* of my Christian experience. I even allowed satan to deceive me and lead me into sin for a while. Fortunately, I repented and Jesus and I went overseas together.

After my discharge from military service, I answered the call to preach God's Word and be His ambassador. After a few years, my wife and I entered a Bible college, which was to provide me with Biblical knowledge that would enable me to preach more effectively. My Bible professors were Godly, holy men. However, they seemed to take the prayer ministry of a minister for granted. They failed to emphasize that prayer and daily communion with the Father were essential if one was to walk in God's holy will and fulfill the call of preaching the Word. They appeared to believe that prayer would naturally become the vital part of the minister's life. The specifics of prayer were never mentioned.

After completing my formal education, I pastored Churches both in Indiana and Michigan, and I also taught English in high school. Yes, I did pray and sought God's will and leadership; nevertheless, prayer had not yet become the heart, the core of my ministry, and life itself. As prayer had not become a daily, meaningful experience, I had not realized that a faithful "quiet time" was actually the most important use of my time. That was a significant truth I was yet to learn.

## THE TURNING POINT

One evening while I was pastoring in Flint, Michigan, I decided to watch TV. As I was flipping through the channels to see what was on, I stopped to listen to a religious program (not realizing God's providential guidance). The year was 1975 or 1976 and Dr. Jack McAlister, the founder of World Literature (now called Every Home for Christ), was urging Christians to commit themselves to at least fifteen minutes per day to the Lord in prayer. That religious program, saturated in the priceless oil of prayer, proved to be the most significant religious program I was ever to hear.

As I listened to the challenge, and as the Holy Spirit tugged at my heart and convicted my soul, I said to myself, "*Yes! I can and should make that commitment!*" That evening, in my heart, I made a vow to God to read the Word and pray daily. Beginning that night, I made both prayer and the Word my priority. Thus, I called the number on the screen and made my prayer commitment. Through the ministry of Every Home for Christ, Jack McAlister, its founder, and Dr. Dick Eastman, who is now the president, my prayer life was radically changed!

I began searching the Bible, seeking out every verse that referred to prayer and its power. Also, I bought every book I could find relating to prayer, especially the books written by Dr. Dick Eastman. When one of his new books came off the press, I bought it.(His books are baptized in the spiritual fire of PRAYER.) I also established a prayer diary and my spiritual growth became a dynamic, purifying fire in my soul.

Each morning became an exciting attraction for me. I no longer entered into a new day thinking basically about my serious responsibilities for the day. I became eager to read and acquaint myself with what God had to say to me which would prepare me for the day. Later God challenged me to read the New Testament and write down every verse that deals with prayer and the power of God. After completing the New Testament from Matthew to Revelation, I had 103 pages written on both sides, which emphasized both prayer and the power of God. Then during my quiet time, the Lord urged me to read daily from the Old Testament, Genesis to Malachi, and once again write down each verse relative to prayer and of God exercising His power.

What a thrilling experience, simply to become acquainted with all the prayers and the power of God in the Old Testament. When I finished I had written on 776 pages, both sides. As I became soaked in the Word of Prayer and reading the prayer books by Dr. Dick Eastman, the consuming fire of prayer burned in every fiber of my soul. I became convinced that if I neglected reading the Word and spending time with my Lord in the chamber of prayer before assuming my daily responsibilities, I was failing as a child of God.

As I read and wrote in my prayer diary and recognized the need of faithful prayer in my own Christian life and in the life of the Church, the Lord began to open the door of opportunity for a teaching ministry. He called and challenged me to the task of pleading with sincere Christians to become Prayer Warriors. Trusting God and His providence, I simply asked Him to open the doors that would permit me to teach prayer workshops, entitled, "Prayer Enrichment Revivals," using the theme "Becoming Prayer Warriors," in the local Church. I became convinced (and I am still convinced) that before the Church of the Lord Jesus Christ can ever witness a revival of evangelism to reach the lost, there must first be a revival of prayer in hearts of God's people. I came to the spiritual understanding that without the incense of the aroma of sincere prayer burning in our own hearts and ascending to God's holy throne, all religious activities of the Church are meaningless and useless. Prayer is and has always been the stimulus factor of the Church. The Holy Book makes that fact clear.

---

*I became convinced (and I am still convinced) that before the Church of the Lord Jesus Christ can ever witness a revival of evangelism to reach the lost, there must first be a revival of prayer in hearts of God's people.*

---

There is the hymn "Higher Ground." The last stanza has these convicting words:

> "I want to scale the utmost height,
> And catch a gleam of glory bright;

But still I'll pray, till heaven I've found,
Lord, lead me on to higher ground!"

That was Moses' desire. It was on Mount Sinai where he scaled the utmost height and caught a gleam of glory bright. God gave these instructions to him:

*Be ready and come up in the morning to Mount Sinai, and present yourself there to Me on the top of the mountain… and he rose up early in the morning and went up on Mount Sinai, as the Lord had commanded him…" (Exodus 34: 2, 4 AMP).*

Dear Prayer Warriors, how strong is your desire for higher ground? Will you pray until heaven you find? To do so, you must, like Moses, go to the mountain! That is what I did in 1975 or 1976. How different my Christian life and ministry have become. What peace I now possess, simply because I start the day with my Lord, spending time with Him first, before entering into anything else! Amen!

This, dear reader, is a very brief synopsis of the spiritual birth of prayer in my own life. May your heart be convicted to a steadfast grip on prayer as you read what I have taught in prayer workshops and may your own quiet time become the spiritual burning fuel that will purify you for each day.

I Peter 4:7 "*But the end of all things is at hand; therefore be serious and watchful in your prayers*" (NKJV).

---

*Spiritual power and victory are available for the local Church. The source is in the hands of those who will commit themselves to become* **PRAYER WARRIORS: SERIOUS MINDED PRAY-ERS!**

---

# PART ONE

# UNDERSTANDING THE GLORIOUS PRIVILEGE OF PRAYER

*"Continue earnestly in prayer, being vigilant in it, with thanksgiving"* Colossians 4:2. (NKJV)

# Chapter 1
## *Understanding the Heart of Prayer*

Several years ago God gave me the following definition of prayer:

*"Prayer is more than uttering words; it is the person himself coming before the throne of God. Prayer is more than saying words. It is my heart becoming one with the heart of God. Prayer is calling God into action to exercise His power and His grace."*

To me, this definition of prayer elevates it from any kind of perfunctory practice and moves one's soul to see and understand prayer from a totally different perspective. Yes, one's prayerful devotion must involve uttering, saying or vocalizing words, but it is much more than that. When I understood the meaning of prayer as a [my] privilege to ascend spiritually to God's holy throne, then prayer became alive in my heart and soul.

**PRAYER IS MY PRIVILEGE TO COME FACE TO FACE WITH GOD HIMSELF AND ENTER BEFORE HIS DIVINE HOLY THRONE!**

When the Holy Spirit made me aware that when I pray, I am spending time with my Saviour, Jesus Christ, that I am also conversing with my Holy Father, that I am also in the company of the Holy Spirit Himself, and that I have approached Their majestic throne, then prayer was no longer a conception to be understood through any intellectual procedure. Communion with the Trinity became a blessed, sacred, meaningful, and personal experience to me.

*To me, prayer is a very personal experience. It allows a finite, limited, earth-bound personality the privilege of communion and fellowship with the infinite God who is omnipotent, omniscient, and omnipresent.*

Exodus 33:11 portrays very vividly that prayer is to be a face to face experience between God and man, one who is a born again person.

*"So the Lord spoke to Moses face to face, as a man speaks to his friend."*

When we Prayer Warriors enter the throne of God, we too are to witness the experience of being with God, "face to face, as a man speaks to a friend."

## PRAYER IS ENTERING THE THRONE ROOM OF HEAVEN.

The word **throne** symbolizes the power, royalty, and sovereignty of a king. Thus, prayer is our blessed privilege of entering and standing before the throne of all royalty.

1. The Lord's throne is enduring and everlasting! (Psalm 9:7) *"But the Lord shall endure forever, He has prepared His throne for judgment."*

2. It is a heavenly throne! (Psalm 11:4) *"The Lord is in His holy temple, the Lord's throne is in heaven. . . ."*

3. God's throne rules over all! (Psalm 103:19) *"The Lord has established His throne in heaven, and His kingdom rules over all."*

4. Isaiah saw and entered the throne-room of God! (Isaiah 6:1) *"In the year that King Uzziah died, I saw the Lord sitting on a throne. . . ."*

5. Micaiah the prophet saw the throne of God! (I Kings 22:19) *"Then Micaiah said, Therefore hear the word of the Lord; I saw the Lord sitting on His throne, and all the host of heaven standing by, on His right hand and on His left."*

6. Stephen, the deacon, saw the throne of God! (Acts 7:55, 56) *But he, being full of the Holy Spirit, gazed into heaven and saw the glory of God, and Jesus standing at the right hand of God, and said, "Look I see the heavens opened and the Son of Man standing at the right hand of God!"*

These meaningful Scriptures declare just what is available to Christians if only we will catch the vision. Prayer is **quiet time**, which means entering the throne room of heaven and enjoying a personal, knowledgeable relationship with the eternal God; The One who created the heavens and the earth (see Genesis 1:1):

*"For He spoke and it was done; He commanded and it stood fast"* (Psalm 33:9).

The greatest privilege God has provided for His children is that we too may experience the joy of having an audience with God even as He sits on His majestic throne!

*"Let us therefore come boldly to the throne of grace that we may obtain mercy and find grace to help in time of need"* Hebrews 4:16.

Several years ago, my wife and I were privileged to go to London, England. Naturally, we were eager to see the Parliament building Buckingham Palace. The street leading up to the palace is painted red, symbolizing royalty. As I saw the red pavement leading up to the home of Queen Elizabeth II, I thought, **Prayer** is the royal avenue that I may travel to reach the heavenly throne of my eternal God! Amen!

The one person who does not want us to pray is, of course, the devil. It is his business to get us so busy in "activities" that we neglect the most important business of all, **prayer!** One of the first books I read about prayer was *No Easy Road*. I read "A most vital but extremely difficult element of the Christian life is prayer."[1]

Yes, dear reader, in prayer, conversing in holy communion and in sensing the presence of the Holy Spirit, coming face to face with the Jehovah God, our hearts do become ONE with the heart of God! Even as the Lord through the prophet Samuel told King Saul, *"...The Lord has sought for Himself a man after His own heart"* (I Samuel 13:14). God is seeking those who desire a heart-to-heart talk with Him and whose heart will become one with His heart, and are thrilled of the privilege of approaching His throne. Yes, travel the blessed street of prayer to God's eternal home!

To pray is a battle against the forces of the devil. He will do all within his evil power to keep you from ascending God's magnificent throne. If the heart of prayer throbs in your heart and you become convicted about prayer as E. M. Bounds, you will become eager to pray.

> "Prayer is not a little habit pinned on to us while we were tied to our mother's apron strings; neither is it a little decent quarter of a minute's grace said over an hour's dinner, but it is a most serious work of our most serious years."[2]

Dear Prayer Warriors, when I was baptized in the holy thought that prayer "is a most serious work of [my] most serious years" and what really happens and takes place when I pray, that I have entered His Divine Throne simply to enjoy His presence, spend time with the

One who saved me from my sins, my prayer life and prayer commitment were revolutionized! Prayer became a meaningful, daily experience. Prayer Warriors, that is what prayer is to be—a daily, glorious experience. Also, God gave me the understanding that not only is prayer communion time, it also summons God into action to exercise and wield His power and His grace. Our minds are too finite to grasp and understand fully the greatness of God's power and ability; but when we refer to God's power, we actually mean what He is capable of doing and accomplishing. The Word of God gives us clear testimony of the awesomeness of His authority.

*"Many, O Lord my God, are the wonders you have done. The things you planned for us; no one can recount to You; were I to speak and tell of them, they would be too many to declare"* (Psalm 40:5 NIV).

God will release His power and authority and marvelous grace when we make it a daily habit to invoke the intimacy of His holy presence! God's control and grace are expressions of His love and righteousness toward His children. It is prayer and the Word that enables God to become a reality to us. The heart of sincere praying is witnessing a **prayer closet experience**, shut out and away from the world and focusing completely upon the One who died for us. This is the faithful experience God desires of His children, for it is essential if there is to be victory over satan's schemes and for the Church to crush his devious plans.

## PRAYER IS THE POWER THAT CALLS GOD INTO ACTION!

When God inspired my soul and spirit to seek Him on His throne, to seek the very heart of God, that my heart may become one with Him through the power of the Holy Spirit, and that my prayers call God Himself into action, I saw and witnessed prayer in a totally different light.

Dear Prayer Warriors, allow the prayerful spirit of David to reach deeply into your soul each morning. I assure you that your experience in your Lord and Christian devotion to Him will become a deeper and meaningful reality.

*"As the deer pants for streams of water, so I long for you, O God"* (Psalm 42:1 NLB).

"Each day is a gift to be opened with prayer."[3]

**PRAYER WARRIORS, REMEMBER THIS TRUTH
AND YOUR PRAYER LIFE WILL BE REVOLUTIONIZED!**

## NOTES

[1] Dr. Dick Eastman, *No Easy Road* (Grand Rapids, MI.: Baker Book House, 1971) (Chap. 2, p. 12). (It was this book and *The Hour that Changes the World*, written also by Dr. Dick Eastman, which convicted me to spend at least an hour with my precious Lord, reading His Word and to pray.)

[2] Ibid., p. 12

[3] *Our Daily Bread*, June, July, August 1995 "On Today's Threshold," July 2.

# Chapter 2
## *Understanding the Sphere of Prayer*

J. Oswald Sanders stated that "it [prayer] can be focused on a single object and it can roam the world."[1] The unlimited scope of prayer may actually be compared to the working of a satellite. As the satellite moves heavenward with its central goal being the realm of heaven itself, prayer, conversing with the eternal God of both heaven and earth, enables us finite creatures, through the spiritual satellite of prayer, to travel to the very heart of God, His heavenly throne. "The Church, the bride, the Eternal Companion is to sit with Him on His throne."[2] In our spirit when we pray, we are sitting with Him on His throne! Amen!

Also this prayer satellite, revolving around the world without any mechanical failures, can penetrate any area of the world. As you center your prayer on your community, family, and, yes, your own or any other nation, God hears the heartbeat of your supplication. Prayer Warriors, as you spend time in your consecrated prayer closet, you can be confident that the range of prayer knows no boundaries, no limitations, no physical hindrances. Your prayer focus has nothing to do with time and space for it is a spiritual experience motivated by the Holy Spirit and the power of God Himself.

The need today is for the Church, God's body of believers on their knees in their prayer closet, to grasp the fact that prayer is directing its face toward the Holy One of the universe. It is entering into a personal, intimate, precious dialogue with Him and praise.

---

*Your prayer focus has nothing to do with time and space; it is a spiritual experience motivated by the Holy Spirit and the power of God Himself.*

---

Daniel is an excellent example of the sphere of prayer: its unlimited dimension. He had been taken captive to Babylon by King Nebuchadnezzar. Even though Daniel was far removed from his homeland, he knew that prayer was the answer for the Jews in exile and for his blessed city Jerusalem. Thus what does he do? Daniel 9:3 records his faith in his Jehovah God and the spiritual energy of prayer:

> *"Then I set my face toward the Lord God to make request by prayer and supplications, with fasting, sackcloth, and ashes."*

Daniel knew the avenue to travel. He was burdened for his nation Israel and he knew God's power to meet the need of the hour and answer his prayer. Even though he was hundreds of miles from the land called Israel, He was not miles away from his God. (As I have read different times, "God is only a prayer away.") Thus, Daniel clothed himself with the burden of fasting, the spirit of humility (sackcloth and ashes). He was serious as he approached the throne of God. In the closet of prayer, Daniel made his requests and supplications to the One who was able and capable of answering his prayer. To him space was not the issue; he was simply to pray and trust his God for the results. Daniel knew that the range of prayer was high, wide, and boundless. E. M. Bounds says it this way: "Prayer must be broad in its scope—it must plead for others. Intercession for others is the hallmark of true prayer. . . . Prayer is the soul of a man stirred to plead with God and men."[3]

My burden and prayer is: "Oh God, awaken the Church of the living God to grasp the fact that You are unlimited, Your power is limitless, and that only our sins separate us from you and become the barrier to answered prayer. May the Church wear the garment of fasting and humility!"

> *"Let God arise, let His enemies be scattered; let those also who hate Him flee before Him. As smoke is driven away, so drive them away..."* (Psalm 68:1, 2a).

Prayer Warriors, David, the man after God's own heart, like Daniel, knew prayer was and is saturated with stuff that makes it real (see Psalm 139). His prayers are prayers of victory; he did not question God's ability. Like Daniel, David has the vision of heaven and the view of God's throne is packed within every word.

The Church, Prayer Warriors, does not exist to be defeated. Because of the scope of prayer, God has ordained it Himself to be the Church's dynamic force and victory. The vision of the Church needs to be the following: see Heaven; see the throne; see God; and claim His authority.

Several years ago, through *Every Home for Christ* and the Holy Spirit, God opened my eyes to the scope of prayer and its dynamic, powerful "up-reach" and "outreach." I grasped the realization that there are no limits to my praying, for God Himself is unlimited. It is my limited vision and faith that are the spiritual problem. How convinced am I that God can, does, and will answer prayer? How serious am I in prayer devotion? Am I determined to make and keep my "prayer-closet" first? Am I earnest enough about prayer, God's divine, holy guidance in my life, that I seek Him and His divine presence first? When I establish in my soul that prayer is truly the answer for all my needs, family needs, my community, city, state, nation, yes, even the world itself, it will move me into a "holy faith" in God and of His unsearchable capability. King David had an understanding of the uniqueness of the Jehovah he served. Listen to his characterization:

> *"Come and see the works of God; He is awesome in His doing toward the sons of men"* (Psalm 66:5).

---

**The vision of the Church needs to be the following: see Heaven; see the throne; see God, and claim His authority.**

---

When we comprehend the force of faith, and allow it to come alive and exciting, we will no longer see obstacles, mountains, and failures; God through prayer will draw us into an intimate relationship with Him. As Prayer Warriors, enjoy this holy **face-to-face** throne-room experience. Let all the limitations to prayer vanish. Why? Because being baptized in the greatness of God, the Unlimited One, the Absolute One, the Glorious One, then when He acts neither satan nor his demons can stand in His way! Hallelujah! He is the spiritual Rock of Gibraltar! It is not satan, but the Trinity who possesses all authority!

> *"And Jesus came and spoke to them, saying, "All authority has been given to Me in heaven and on earth"* (Matthew 28:18).

*When we comprehend the force of faith, and allow it to come alive in the depth of our soul, we will no longer see obstacles, mountains, and failures.*

Because of this unique supremacy of God, each Prayer Warrior is able to roam the world in prayer while sitting, kneeling, and walking around in his own prayer closet. Understand the sphere of prayer and the victory established through it, and you will unconditionally become a serious-minded Prayer Warrior! Oh for us to embrace the spiritual insight of prayer as David did:

> "I will cry out to God Most High, to God who performs all things for me! He shall send from heaven and save me; He reproaches the one who would swallow me up. Selah. God shall send forth His mercy and His truth" (Psalm 57:2, 3).

When you grasp and understand prayer as David did, you will become a Serious-Minded Prayer Warrior!

Prayer Warriors, prayer is serious business! Its scope is unending. When we really comprehend prayer and the forceful power of its strength, energy, and outreach, we will pray, pray, and keep on praying!

### TRAVELING ON MY KNEES

Last night I took a journey to
A land far 'cross the seas;
I didn't go by boat or plane,
I traveled on my knees.

I saw so many people there
In deepest depths of sin,
And Jesus told me I should go
That these were souls to win.

But I said, "Jesus, I can't go
And work with such as these."
He answered quickly, "Yes you can
By traveling on your knees."

> He said, "You pray; I'll meet the need,
> You call and I will hear;
> Be concerned about lost souls,
> Of those both far and near."
>
> And so I tried it, knelt in prayer,
> Gave up some hours of ease;
> I felt the Lord right by my side
> While traveling on my knees.
>
> I said, "Yes, Lord, I have a job
> My desire Thy will to please;
> I can go and heed Thy call
> By traveling on my knees."
>
> By Sandra Goodwin

Prayer Warriors, we can remain at home, go to our prayer chamber and serve the Lord of heaven as Missionary Prayer Warriors. **Let's do it!!**

## NOTES

[1] J. Oswald Sanders, *The Joy of Following Jesus*, 1990, 1994 by Moody Bible Institute of Chicago. Originally published as *Shoe-Leather Commitment*, this book, in a revised edition, is available from Moody Press and through bookstores under the title *Spiritual Discipleship*, Ch. 13, "The Disciple's Prayer Life," p. 97.

[2] Paul E. Billheimer, *Destined for The Throne*, Christian Lit. Crusade, Inc., Fort Washington, PA., 1975, p. 27

[3] Dick Eastman, *The Hour That Changes the World*, Baker Book House, Grand Rapids, MI., 1978, p. 77.

# Chapter 3
## *Personal Prayer Evaluation*

A serious-minded prayer warrior is not one who takes the privilege of prayer for granted. Still there must be a *"watch and pray,"* a "spiritual alertness," for it is the devil's business to cause one to become so occupied with the *"things of life"* that would cause him or her to neglect the priceless time of communion and fellowship with their Jehovah God. Thus, in this chapter let us take a Personal Prayer Evaluation examination.

The word *personal* means intimate, the inner being of the person, that which is private. The word *evaluation* means the act of determining the worth of something. That something may be that of an object or the stewardship of your time; that is, the time involved for any activity. Involvement demands time; consequently, the question may well be is that particular activity worthy of the time it demands? The prayer closet! This requires time that is to be devoted completely with and to the Prince of Peace; let's visit the depth of your heart to determine your attitude toward this use of your valuable time. Let's take a very personal journey and observe just how your spiritual stewardship measures up.

### AT THIS PRESENT TIME

As you read this sentence right now, how do you characterize your own personal prayer life? How meaningful is prayer to you? Do you consider prayer to be an essential, holy activity for your daily life? Is it worthy of the time demanded? How would you answer this first question?

1. My daily prayer life is weak! I say **grace** at the table, when called on at Church for **public prayer,** or when a *crisis* arises. Other than these occasions I find no reason to pray.

2. Should Christians say grace prior to eating? The answer, of course, is Yes! In fact, Jesus is our best Example to teach us the importance of expressing grace prior to a meal. Matthew 14:17-21

(NIV) records the scene of Jesus feeding five thousand people, men, women, and children. The thought of feeding that many staggered the minds of His apostles. (It does mine also.)

Jesus simply took five loaves of bread and two fish, which were supplied to Him by a small lad, and multiplied them into abundance and the apostles fed the hungry. What a miracle Jesus accomplished! To me, Prayer Warriors, the significance is more than the miracle itself. What did Jesus do prior to the multiplication of bread and fish? He said **grace**! He spent a few moments with His Father (that is what grace is, a moment of time spent with the Father to thank Him for what we have to eat). Amen!

*"And he directed the people to sit down on the grass. Taking the five loaves and the two fish and looking up to heaven, he gave thanks [Jesus said grace] and broke the loaves"* (v. 19).

Yes, we Christians are to say grace preceding a meal; but if that is the extent of our prayer life, if you pray only to say **"table grace,"** then your Christian commitment to prayer is extremely weak. Again, Jesus is our prime Example.

*"Immediately Jesus made his disciples get into the boat and go on ahead of him to Bethsaida, while he dismissed the crowd. After leaving them, he went up on a mountainside to pray"* (Mark 6:45-46, NIV).

---

**A protracted time of prayer with His Father was indispensable to Jesus!**

---

Jesus had given thanks to His Father, completed the miracle, and met the physical need of the people. Such an enormous miracle, which testifies of His stupendous authority, did not exalt Jesus; that is, He didn't feel those few moments of table-grace were sufficient. He dismissed both the people and His apostles,

*"And when He had sent the multitudes away, He went up on the mountain by Himself to pray"* (Matthew 14:22 NIV).

Jesus would not allow even the ministry of doing good rob Him of the time with His Father. He knew He needed more prayer than simply saying grace. Protracted time with His Holy Father was indispensable. To Jesus, the time spent in prayer was the occasion for inner strength and spiritual nourishment.

*Jesus never neglected His "prayer closet" experience! Can we Prayer Warriors afford to do less?*

Is **public prayer** important and should it be a strong ingredient in the life of the Christian? Again, the answer is yes! The question, nonetheless, to be asked is this: Is that basically the only occasion for you to pray? If so, how long has it been since the pastor, Sunday School teacher, or any other Christian leader asked you to pray? Furthermore, many pastors never call on their lay people to pray. For one reason or another they seem to prefer to pray all the prayers associated with public worship. Thus, again, if the only time you pray, talk to the blessed Lord, is when asked to, no doubt you do not go to the throne very often. It certainly will not be a daily experience; your understanding of worship with God is, and will continue to be, weak and basically meaningless to you.

It is interesting to me that as Jesus' apostles came upon Him while He was praying and listening to Him, they were convicted of the weakness of their own prayer life. Also, I am confident, that they sensed power, an intimacy, and a Godly inspiration when Jesus prayed which was lacking in their own prayer life. Let their sincere request which they made to Jesus sink deeply into your own soul. I assure you that as you grow in the knowledge, understanding, and privilege of prayer, your prayer commitment will be anything but weak or anemic.

> *One day Jesus was praying in a certain place [His prayer closet]. When he finished, one of his disciples said to him, "Lord, teach us to pray, just as John taught his disciples"* (Luke 11:1 NIV).

"Jesus was praying"! meaning, when the apostles approached Him, they did not disturb Him, for they saw that His activity was prayer. They observed their Master engaged in an intense, serious conversation with His and their heavenly Father. No doubt, these dedicated apostles were well acquainted with the prayers of Moses, Joshua, and Daniel, just to name a few; but when they listened to Jesus' prayer, they became keenly aware of a character and depth of prayer they had never beheld before. Thus, their prayer request: "*Lord, teach us to pray.*" Jesus listened to their request and taught them the Model Prayer.

Dear pray-er, if your prayer life at times becomes rather weak and meaningless, read the prayer Jesus taught His disciples. Don't just read it; prayerfully study it and allow its meaning and directive absorb your soul. For then you will, without fail, grow beyond the few moments you allow for saying grace; or the waiting until you have been asked to pray during public worship.

Continuing with this prayer evaluation or the attitude toward prayer, do you only pray when a need or crisis arises? The word **need** simply means that which is considered to be necessary or the lack of something. The word **crisis** means facing situations that are determined to be crucial. One Church member, facing a rather serious point in his life, said, "I normally only pray at Church, but this is serious enough that I have been praying at home." God, our Father, help us! Prayer is not an ingenious way to enable us to get what we want or feel we need.

You may inquire: "Shouldn't Christians pray to the Lord when specific needs in their lives are apparent; or when facing serious situations which may even involve life or death?" The answer, of course, is a big, healthy yes! Both the Old and New Testaments record both needs and critical surroundings that provoke the need and spirit of prayer.

Abraham, that patriarch of the Old Testament, the father of the Hebrew race, certainly was committed to prayer as he sensed his own helplessness. (To me, that is the heart of praying about **needs:** realizing our own helplessness.) At the age of seventy-five, God spoke to Abraham and challenged him to his most grave task.

> "*So Abram departed as the Lord had spoken to him, and Lot went with him. And Abram was seventy-five years old when he departed from Haran. Then the Lord appeared to Abram and said, "To your descendants I will give this land." And there he built an altar to the Lord, who had appeared to*

him" (Genesis 12:4, 7).

Abram built an altar. Why? I believe he was focusing on the tremendous responsibility God had placed upon him at the age of seventy-five. This was a sobering experience for him; and he was admitting his own helplessness and inability to fulfill the challenge. Furthermore, I believe Abram saw the altar as an occasion to worship God; and, Prayer Warriors, that is exactly the heart of prayer! Yes, there are needs and crises to talk to God about and take them to the Throne. The point is this. If we commune with God only during the severe times in our lives, then we don't have an appreciation of the blessing and fellowship available to us as children of God. It is important to remember daily that we Christians are God's adopted children and He desires communion and fellowship with His children.

Moses, that prophet of God who was a humble servant of the Lord, faced horrible, hopeless trials during his journey with the children of Israel. He endured periods of scraps and difficult hardships. He too, like Abraham, knowing his powerlessness to accomplish the formidable task God had placed upon him, called upon his Jehovah God to supply what was lacking. In short, Moses sought God's directive for himself and the Israelites. For example, when there was no water to drink for Israel, it was a time of crisis. Israel was blaming Moses. Observe the scene:

> "When they came to Marah, they could not drink its water because it was bitter. . . . So the people grumbled against Moses, saying, "What are we to drink?" Then Moses cried out to the Lord. . . ." (Exodus 15: 23-25 NIV).

Moses prayed and God came to the rescue and met the crisis. There was an urgent need; the Israelites needed drinking water. The question again is: Why did Moses pray? The answer is his defenselessness against Israel. He could not supply or produce water. Thus he sought the One who could. It was a time of crisis. Moses' arrogant attitude of self-sufficiency was gone. He had become humble in spirit, dependent upon his God. The great Jehovah, witnessing the humble, helpless spirit of Moses, characterized him with the following declaration:

> (Now the man Moses was very humble, more than all men

*who were on the face of the earth.)"* (Numbers 12: 3).

There are many such examples when hopelessness is evident and there is the feeling of being totally destitute. Yes! There are times for crises prayers; and I want to emphasize that all of life is so unpredictable, we are so finite, we are to pray daily to God. Not merely when we are confronted with problems, for God is our Strength in all life situations and decisions. We need Him every hour of the day! At the threat of overstating the point, I want to say again that if prayer to God is made solely at mealtime, or during worship, or when being confronted with the crises of life, our understanding of communion with our blessed Lord is very limited. There is the failure of a heartfelt appreciation to God or the understanding of prayer in our daily lives.

Question: Does this second evaluation declare accurately your spiritual temperature relative to sincere prayer?

2. My prayer life is almost **non-existent**. I rarely take time to pray. I'm busy and prayer seems abstract and non-effective to me!

To how many Christians does this evaluation apply? No doubt, it must grieve the heart of God, for He knows exactly how many who have this attitude toward prayer. Let us examine some of the key words within this evaluation. Prayer is almost **non-existent.** Such a spirit toward prayer speaks very clearly of the place of prayer in the person's life. Very little consideration is ever given to prayer, and surely there is no such experience as the prayer closet. If there is prayer at all, it is no more than a brief, fleeting moment. The prefix **non** means not; therefore, there is practically no prayer thought in the mind of the professed believer. The word **existent** means being or alive; an "almost non-existent prayer life" indicates the comprehension of who God is and of His love and power is nil. The place of prayer as worship and communion with God has been buried under the rubble of carnality.

Next is the reason, better still the excuse, of a neglected prayer life. The Christian claims to be too busy, meaning there is so much to do which demands time. The reasoning is this—time is such a precious commodity that praying in the prayer closet robs the person of valuable time which must be used for that which is more vital! What is meaningful to such a person is work activity; this means that energy is applied in the occupation of materialism. Laziness is not an aspect of his life, but what is essential to life is absent. Actually the busyness of life isn't what is stealing the person of a meaningful, prayerful experience. The problem is spiritual blinders on the eyes, a failure to see, grasp, or to know that prayer is more than saying words and then moving on to busyness. It is worship, time devoted to and giving oneself to God. It is seeing ourselves, as we truly are totally ignorant to function according to the will of our heavenly Father. What would happen in the lives of Christians and the Church if they genuinely prayed the prayer David did?

> "*Show me Your ways, O Lord; teach me Your paths. Lead me in Your truth and teach me, For You are the God of my salvation; on You I wait all the day*" (Psalm 25:4-5).

I am sorry to admit there are those who profess to be Christians who feel prayer is non-effective. Several years ago a dear lady whom I had known since a teen-ager said to me in desperation: "I don't know of one prayer I ever prayed that God answered." How dreadful! Surely God had answered some of her sincere prayers. Maybe she had simply forgotten. (Later I shall encourage keeping a prayer diary. It is a fantastic method for remembering the prayers God has answered.)

This attitude means the person, in his opinion, has never seen answered prayers. To him or her there are no results to praying. Prayer fails! Why take time, wasting priceless time in a practice that brings no practical known facts? Nothing ever appears to happen anyway. There is no power evident, which means there are no answers being produced. A few years ago I was teaching one of my prayer workshops, "Becoming Prayer Warriors." The young pastor of the Church was excited about what I was sharing. He challenged another pastor to daily, faithful prayer. To his amazement, the pastor told him: "I am just too busy to take time for extended prayer."

This is just another example that even many pastors feel their work in the Lord is so time-consuming that they are too busy for prayer. What is sad is the fact that the ministry of the Lord is so urgent and yet so many fail to realize that spiritual success rests with the power and strength of the Lord. He is the One who sees that victory is won and prayer plays a significant role for such spiritual victory to become a reality! Many of our pastors, however, have lost sight that His work of salvation is accomplished through Him, not through their human ingenuity.

The word *effective* means the act of producing, accomplishing; in short, it means getting things done. Because the person accuses prayer of being abstract and non-effective and not able to accomplish any specific fulfillment, there is a total dependence on self. This attitude of **self-ability**, possessing no faith in prayer and its power, causes one actually to reject prayer and to believe that the challenges of life are met and conquered through self-initiative. The conclusion from these two evaluations is that there is a complete failure of understanding the heart and privilege of prayer. They interpret any occasion given to prayer being aimless, empty, pointless; thus, a waste of valuable time. Self is the means of getting things done, not through the abstractness or non-effectiveness of prayer. (If you desire insight to prayer, read the Psalms. I call the book of Psalms the Prayer Book of the Bible!)

Now let us examine the last evaluation relative to prayer. My heartfelt prayer is that as you read this third appraisal, you will be able to mark a big check in the affirmative.

3. My prayer life is a consistent, meaningful **experience**. I take time to pray daily, at a particular place. It is my time to dismiss all earthly busyness from my mind and rejoice in communion with my Lord. Realizing my own defenselessness for the day, the prayer closet is my sanctuary. As I breathe in the spiritual power and energy of God's power and presence, I am then prepared to resist satan's evil tactics and devious schemes against me and face the formidable task of the day knowing that God

*". . . is my rock and my fortress and my deliverer; My God, my strength, in whom I will trust; my shield and the horn of my salvation, my stronghold. I will call upon the Lord, who is worthy to be praised; So shall I be saved from my enemies"* (Psalm 18:2-3).

If you, dear Prayer Warriors, can say that these words depict your spirit toward prayer, then you are surely enjoying the rich experience of spending time with your holy Master. I use the preposition *with*, which means association or accompanying, for that is the cornerstone of prayer; that is, being close to the Lord as you talk to each other.

The word **consistent** indicates a relationship to prayer, habitual and not a hit-and-miss occasion. Prayer seeks God's divine strength and presence for the day; it is requesting His guidance to lead you during the day. Consistency in prayer results when there is the awareness of helplessness and the need of total dependence upon God. A consistent, meaningful prayer life means that as you face and enter into the responsibilities of a new day, you desire the guidance of the Holy Spirit to surround you and walk with you and secure you with His Godly protection. Because of this spiritual philosophy toward prayer, you then take time, make time, and carve out the time needed to be with your holy Father. You stubbornly refuse to allow daily activities to become your priority and claim possession of your time and steal away your prayer closet experience God desires to have with you. You are dedicated to the conviction that you must see the face of God first and then you are ready and fortified for the day. Oh! for us to lock it into our memory that God's longing is for His children to seek His holy, righteous face.

*"When You said, 'Seek my face,' my heart said to You, 'Your face, Lord, I will seek'"* (Psalm 27:8).

After teaching one of my prayer workshops, I received a letter from a lady who wrote: "I have found out that prayer is more important than 'Good Morning, America.'" I say, "Amen!" Again after my teaching that time in prayer with our blessed, divine Omnipotent God is not being squandered, a pastor wrote these words which one of his Church ladies stated to him: "It (prayer commitment) had changed her life."

Yes, the opportunity of prayer, a time of conversation with the eternal One of the universe, should be a consistent, exciting experience. In fact, it must be if we expect to become one of God's Prayer Warriors! Don't allow the first two evaluations to characterize your prayer life. Don't allow your Christian life to become that shallow. Claim and live by the third evaluation. You will witness a spiritual revolution in your own spirit and your life in Christ will assume a new meaning and purpose. Be convicted, Dear Prayer Warriors, to this quotation:

**"To be a Christian without prayer is no more possible than to be alive without breathing."**

Many of us need to pray this prayer: "Dear God, teach me to plug into Your power."

*Begin each new day in the "prayer closet"! God is there waiting for you!*

If you haven't yet checked the third evaluation in your heart, the question to you is this, "What is hindering you the most from having a rejoicing, consistent, and meaningful prayer life?" Remember, the problem isn't with God. It is we who are committing the failure. Don't permit things, activities, or obligations to become roadblocks to hinder your most indispensable business—devoting time in the Prayer Closet! **Begin each new day in the "prayer closet"! God is waiting for You!**

# Chapter 4
## *The Privilege To Pray Motivates Serious-Minded Pray-ers*

Lord Alfred Tennyson said: "More things are wrought [accomplished] by prayer than this world dreams of." Jesus Christ, God's divine Son, is even more specific to the results and power of prayer. He said:

> "Ask, and you will be given what you ask for. Seek, and you will find. Knock, and the door will be opened. For everyone who asks, receives. Anyone who seeks, finds. If only you will knock, the door will open" (Matthew 7:7-8 TLB).

**"Ask, Seek, Knock!"** These are three powerful, active verbs that speak loudly and clearly that our heavenly Father is as close as a whisper when we pray. He never slumbers, never leaves us stranded, but He watches over His children and waits for them to ask, seek or knock!

> "He will never let me stumble, slip or fall. For he is always watching, never sleeping" (Psalm 121:3, TLB).
> "For the eyes of the Lord are intently watching all who live good lives, and he gives attention when they cry to him" (Psalm 34:15, TLB).

Thus, the need today is for us all to become spiritually attentive to prayer through the eyes of the Lord. It is He who encourages prayer; He desires our communion with Him. He is waiting for us to **ask, seek, and knock!** God is always there, never sleeping! never indifferent to the necessities of His blessed children! Indeed He who watched over and cared for and guarded over His children Israel, definitely gives careful attention to those who are committed to prayer. What a privilege prayer is. It ushers the pray-er into the presence of and before the very throne and majesty of God himself. The word **privilege** means "a special right, or immunity granted to a person or group."[1] Our heavenly Father has granted us the most sparkling privilege there is—the dynamics of Prayer! Communion!

Fellowship! Therefore, Prayer Warriors, as the Lord Himself encourages and exhorts us to ask, seek, and knock, and then as He has promised to hear when we ask, to provide when we seek, and then to open the windows of heaven when we knock, can you think of any logical reason why the children of God should not become motivated to be serious-minded pray-ers? To be **serious-minded** is having a serious disposition or trend of thought. The word **serious** means being sober-minded or in earnest. Paul tells us just how earnest a Prayer Warrior should be.

*"Don't be weary in prayer; keep at it; watch for God's answers and remember to be thankful when they come"* (Colossians 4:2, TLB).

The devotional booklet, *Our Daily Bread*, tells the story that exemplifies being serious-minded: A group of boys arrived at a stream with their rods and reels and fancy flies. They thrashed the water as they joked and laughed, casting and reeling in repeatedly but catching nothing. Another boy was also there fishing. Every so often he pulled up a fish. Finally one of the fellows shouted, "How do you do it? We've got special flies but we're not catching anything." The boy looked up long enough to reply, "I'm fishing for fish—you're fishing for fun."[2] Definitely this lad was serious about his fishing.

## OUR PRAYER-TIME IS OUR PRIVILEGED TIME.

I am persuaded, Prayer Warriors, that one of the greatest urgencies facing the Church is for busy pastors, busy lay people to become motivated to prayer. I heard Kenneth Copeland over TV say the following about the word **motivation**: "It has the word **motor** within it." Motivation is the "motor" needed to cause the Church to see that prayer is indispensable. In fact, Christendom itself must awaken spiritually and catch the vision and insight of prayer and realize the power, results, glory, and blessings that are available. When we ask, seek, and knock, Jesus is saying, "Yes"! How may I help you?" When the Church, God's people, awaken to the fact that our prayer-time with God is actually a privilege, then we will recognize prayer being our "privileged-time." Jesus Himself knew that prayer was a must if His Church was to survive and witness victory. Too many of us professed Christians, like the apostles, would rather sleep than watch with the Lord (see Mark 14:37-38). Jesus knew that He could not abuse the privilege He had of talking to His Father. He recognized that His time spent with Him was the most effective way of accomplishing what His Father wanted Him to consummate. Jesus never neglected this gracious right He had. My burden is that if the Church doesn't awaken to this holy privilege, we are doomed to failure. It is through prayer the Church receives its orders and specific directions which enables it to be an effective, spiritual organism living in the heart of a sinful world!

Prayer is not some intricate ritual to be followed religiously. It is praising the Lord for who He is and what He has done for us, confessing and acknowledging our sin to Him, and in our hearts admitting our own helplessness and total dependence on Him. When we perceive prayer in this radiant glow, then the blessing of prayer will come. There will be an eagerness to begin each day with the Lord for then we will see prayer being the privilege it is.

The Lord taught Moses the importance of spending time with Him. Listen to the specific instructions God gave to him.

> *"So be ready in the morning, and come up in the morning to Mount Sinai, and present yourself to Me there on the top of the mountain"* (Exodus 34:2).

God was encouraging Moses, "Don't be lazy, nonchalant, an indifferent servant of Mine. Moses, I have some very important words for you. For you to hear them, it is productive that you 'be ready in the morning, come up . . . to Mount Sinai.'" That is a good place for us to meet. Moses' motivation, his spiritual "motor," was such a driving force that he simply spent forty days in communion with his Jehovah God. If we Christians will only open our eyes to the favor God has granted us through the avenue of prayer, that He is patiently waiting eagerly for this dialogue between Himself and His children, and that the "prayer closet" is a blessed, holy, glorious place, and allow prayer to become a daily experience with Him, then a serious-minded spirit and attitude will be the spiritual response. God's promises (I read that the Bible contains more than ten thousand promises) should be enough to motivate and challenge us to pray and to keep on praying. Lock in to God's promises and the neglect of prayer will then be nil. Oh! for us to be convicted to the fact that spending specific time with the Eternal God is a blessed, humbling, and worshipful experience. When we come to that appreciation of prayer, we will everyday be motivated to go to the mountain, as

Moses did, to be with God in prayer!

Yes! We will say, *"Prayer-time is privileged time."* Prayer is our gracious honor to kneel before our merciful, divine, and glorious Father!

> *"Come, kneel before the Lord our Maker, for he is our God. We are his sheep and he is our Shepherd. Oh, that you would hear him calling you today and come to him"* (Psalm 95:6-7, TLB)!

This one plea from the Lord should be enough to motivate us to pray, pray, and to keep on praying. The burden of my soul and prayer is that as you complete this chapter, you will vow in your heart that prayer will become your most important motivation and appointment (in Part Three I will go into detail of the appointment). May God's blessings rest with you as you read chapter five, "God and Prayer First."

## NOTES

[1]*Webster's 11 New Riverside Dictionary*, Revised Edition, "The Foremost Paperback Dictionary," Houghton, Mifflin Co., Boston, New York, Copyright 1996.

[2]Paul R. VanGorder, *Our Daily Bread*, RBC Ministries, "Serious About Fishing," 5/11/91.

# Chapter 5
## Seek God Through Prayer First

*"But my eyes are fixed on You, O Sovereign Lord"*
*(Psalm 141:8a, NIV).*

 The word **first** is a one-syllable word, possessing only five letters, yet its definition is basic to what is considered to be significantly important. It means **priority**. For example, when a man and a woman marry each other, they have declared their love and devotion for and to each other. Their marriage vows are not to their friends, relatives, or even to their parents. They have declared their sacred pledge to one another, meaning that their love is centered toward each other; that is, they view each other as being first place, and this priority establishes their marriage relationship. In like manner, as a Christian is introduced to the **Godhead**—God the Father, Jesus the Son, and the Holy Spirit who is God's power in action who saves us from and out of our sins, which is called the **new birth**—it is critical for the new Christian and older Christians alike to learn who is to be **first**. David, realizing the wickedness in the world and the need for spiritual safekeeping, understood the meaning of who should, in fact, must be, first or have priority in his life, for as quoted above, he said,

 *"But my eyes [my focus, my mind, and my attention] are fixed on You, O Sovereign Lord."*

 *"My voice You shall hear in the morning, O Lord; In the morning I will direct it to You, and I will look up"* (Psalm 5:3).

 There is a serious urgency for the Church to awaken to the understanding that it is God Himself who is to be first, rather than getting lost in the materialistic aspect of this fleeting life. David had established a priority as to what or who was to be first in his life. He stated clearly his mind-set for each new day. To him, God was to be his priority; therefore, He made God and prayer his morning activity. He said, "In the morning I will direct it [meaning his prayer] to You."

 Prayer Warriors, if we set our eyes and fasten them steadfastly on our Sovereign God, then prayer will also be first in our lives. Oh! To awaken from a night of peaceful sleep and see the face of God through His Word and prayer, before seeing the jungle world we

Christians must face each day. When we become fired up about who God is and fix our eyes on Him, then we will recognize that He is capable of meeting every need. It all begins with reading and listening to His Word and then the holy privilege of our articulating our love for Him.

Matthew 6: 31-33 (TLB) are the words of Jesus instructing the apostles about the right attitude toward life itself: what should occupy the mind when facing each new day. It is a Godly approach that, perceives the One who has control over each day, that is, how to enter it.

> *So don't worry at all about having enough food and clothing. Why be like the heathen? For they take pride in all these things and are deeply concerned about them. But your heavenly Father already knows perfectly well that you need them, and He will give them to you if you give Him first place in your life and live as He wants you to.*

Yes, our heavenly Father is certainly aware of our every need; and He urges us, even as He warned His apostles, not to pattern their priorities after what the heathen considered vital or their earthly wants. He shared with them the depth of His Father's knowledge; in fact, He already knows perfectly well that you need them—food and clothing. Jesus called them to anchor their lives on the priority of life—**"give Him first place."**

Prayer Warriors, first place means starting the day with the One who already knows your every need. Jesus' emphasis is communion and fellowship. "I am the One who hears and answers your prayers; thus let Me be first place in and with you." The **new birth experience** is a marvelous, spiritual adventure, but Jesus does not want us to feel that one face-to-face encounter is sufficient for all of the Christian life. Be motivated to see the face of the eternal God daily; seek to live in His presence every day; spend time with the Lord without fail. That is exactly what He desires from His children. Jesus is saying, "Don't fret and worry; trust Me; look to Me; I am sufficient to supply your every lack, but make Me your priority for each and every day!"

Again let the words of David arouse your prayer commitment:

*"When You said, 'Seek My face,' my heart said to You, 'Your face, Lord, I will seek'"* (Psalm 27:8).

I believe that is one of God's greatest cravings. That is, that His spiritual offspring would crave to seek His holy face in the prayer closet in preparation for the day's responsibilities. If one's daily devotion of Bible reading and prayer is ever to become a meaningful, blessed delight, then one must first yearn for the face of God Himself. What do you anticipate seeing when you awaken each new morning? God says, "I hunger for you to seek Me and spend time with Me first."

## WHY SHOULD GOD BE FIRST?

We are such small, finite, insignificant creatures on this earth. Yet God loves us! We may consider ourselves bright, intelligent, and full of "know how," but the truth is we are bound by "natural law"; that is, we are earth-bound creatures. God, however, is infinite, endless, and non-measurable. We have the ability to do and to build; God has the unique ability to create. Moreover, it was He who burst through the veil of endless eternity and spoke time and space and earth into existence:

*"In the beginning God created the heavens and the earth"* (Genesis 1:1).

*"For He spoke, and it was done; He commanded, and it stood fast"* (Psalm 33:9).

What power! God was not lost within the majestic, colorful thread that runs through the rainbow. (He has never been lost!) He is the potent One who spoke the rainbow into existence. He even established a covenant with Noah, which was symbolized by the witness of the rainbow. Speaking to Noah after the flood, God assured him that the earth would be spared and never again endure the devastation of destructive flooding it had endured.

*"I set My rainbow in the cloud, and it shall be for the sign of the covenant between Me and the earth"* (Genesis 9:13).

God is the Source, Foundation, and the Energy that thrives throughout the universe. It is He and He alone who gives reason and perception to the creation of the heavenly and the earth below. Therefore, Prayer Warriors, see God first. Get a glimpse of His creative power, focus first your eyes of faith and your heart and soul on God and praise Him for His miraculous power! King David's heartthrob was for God; he stated:

*"My eyes are ever on the Lord . . ."* (Psalm 25:15, NIV).

"My eyes . . . on the Lord. . . ." Oh, for that to become the heartthrob of the Christian Church! If we Christians craved the presence of God as Dawson Trotman did, what a spiritual transformation it would witness. During the "roaring twenties" this young man was converted to the new life in Jesus Christ; later he founded The Navigators. The following is a brief caption of his desire to see the face of God. The year is 1929. At the age of 23, the dominant theme of Dawson's life was prayer. Prayer alone, with another, or with a group. Prayer early and late.

> "Saturday, August 24—We had a wonderful meeting at San Pedro. 20 Navigators (boys) and Jr. Fishermen, 5 Sr. Fishermen. Afterwards Ed, Bill, Jim, Walter, and I had a prayer meeting lasting until about 11 o'clock. . . Jim, Walt, and I continued **all night** [emphasis mine] in prayer to God.
>
> Sunday, August 25—At 6 a.m. we were met by five others and had a prayer meeting on the hill. Preached . . . at Harbor City Methodist Church. Evening, led young people's meeting at Wilmington Methodist Church.
>
> Wednesday, August 28—Had a talk with Miss Mills after prayer meeting. . . .
>
> Thursday, August 28—Then a prayer-meeting on the hill—alone with God."[1]

"Alone with God"! When Dawson Trotman met the Master, he simply couldn't get enough of His presence. All throughout the day from morning until late at night, he sought the face of his Master. He spent much time in prayer with others; yet, like Jesus, he desired to be alone in prayer with his Lord. Oh, what God could do with us, the Church, if only there were that hunger, that motivating desire to see His glorious face!

## THE FACE OF GOD IS THE POWER OF HIS PRESENCE

Serious-minded Prayer Warriors desire God's divine presence and intimacy more than anything else. David characterized this desire, his craving and longing for the face, the presence of God in his life. He grew from the scene of a thirsty deer to drive the point home to others:

> "As the deer pants for water, so I long for you, O God. I thirst for God, the living God" (Psalm 42:1-2, TLB).

Oh! for us to have the instinct of a delicate deer. When it becomes weak, tired, and thirsty because of its galloping along the trail, its instinct is to find the water brook and drink out of its refreshing stream until the thirst is satisfied. Jesus, speaking to the multitude, said,

> "Blessed are those who hunger and thirst for righteousness, for they shall be filled" (Matthew 5:6).

Oh, for us to grasp and really comprehend what it means to hunger and thirst for God, His holy, hallowed presence! Such thirst and hunger are satisfied as we read, study, memorize, and apply the Word; and then spread our souls before God in sincere, dedicated prayer.

The **prayer closet** is the refreshing stream, our spiritual water hole. It is here that the face of God emerges and His presence and the power of His glory become evident. Our daily and predominant thirst before we leave our habitation for the chores of the day should ever be the same as David's:

> "O God, You are my God; **early** [emphasis mine] will I seek You; my soul thirsts for You; my flesh longs for You in a dry and thirsty land where there is no water" (Psalm 63:1).

> Your heart, O Lord, says, "Come and talk with Me, O My people"! And my heart responds, "Yes, Lord, I am coming."[2]

Prayer Warriors, if you are guilty of seeking after that which does not have eternal value more than the face of the infinite God, you are missing the spiritual bull's eye of life itself. Pursue in your spirit and soul God's divine face and presence before seeking anything else. The prayer closet is the altar, the water brook where you can go and drink of the grandeur of His holy presence, and experience the genuine praise within the gateway of heaven itself.

It grieves the heart of our heavenly Father, if we become so engrossed with the elements of this perishable world that we neglect to seek after, and crave, and strive for the purity of His face and Godly company first. For years I have heard it said that there is the danger of becoming so heavenly minded that we are no earthly good. I don't believe that is the problem. To me, just the opposite is the case. That is, the Christians and the Church have become so earthly minded that we are not heavenly minded. How much of God, heaven, eternity, the glory of God's presence, or even a throbbing desire for His Word and prayer, enter our callous, carnal hearts? Oh, for God's Word, His presence, and the conversation of prayer to possess and occupy our minds that we will picture ourselves being in the presence of the Master as a deer drinking at the water brook. Jesus is the Water of Life; and the Word and prayer are the vital stream in which we are privileged to drink. The question is, are we going to the "stream" for that refreshing drink before facing "the dry desert of the world"?

*The law of the LORD is perfect, reviving the soul. The statutes of the LORD are trustworthy, making wise the simple.* (Psalm 19:7 NIV).

Prayer is a spiritual business from beginning to end, and its aim and object end not with man, but reaches to God [His Face] Himself.[3]

Spiritual power, direction, strength, and fortitude are all found as we feed on God's Word and spend time in the throne room with the King of kings and the Lord of lords! Yes, as Spurgeon said, "Prayer is a spiritual business. . . ," and there is a drastic need for a generation of serious-minded Prayer Warriors to come forth in the land, who will arise early, seek the face of God, and then go into the market place of life and, like Jesus, go "in the power of the Spirit."

*"Then Jesus, being filled with the Holy Spirit, returned from the Jordan and was led by the Spirit into the wilderness... Then Jesus returned in the power of the Spirit to Galilee, and news of Him went out through all the surrounding region."* (Luke 4: 1, 14).

As you complete this chapter, I pray that your heart will be moved and convicted and you will say, "Yes, Lord, I want to see Your face first before I see the face of the world"!

## NOTES

[1]Betty Lee Skinner, *Daws: A Man Who Trusted God*, Copyright 1974, Zondervan Publishing House, Grand Rapids, MI., p. 50
[2]The Author
[3]Warren W. Wiersbe, *Classic Sermons of Prayer*, Hendrickson Publishers, Inc. Copyright 1987, C. H. Spurgeon, "The Throne of Grace," p. 27.

# Chapter 6
## *More Seeking God Through Prayer First*

There are many Prayer Warriors in both the Old and New Testaments one may view to determine the role of prayer in their lives. Let's look at Paul; both prayer and the pursuit of the Jehovah God were significantly important to him.

The Apostle Paul, a prisoner in Rome, because of his ministry of the gospel and faith in the Jehovah God, did not allow it to hinder his spirit of worshiping the true and living God. (I believe Paul was in the spirit of worship even while he was writing to young Timothy even though he was a prisoner). As he reflected on the holy nature of God, he burst forth in exuberant praise and exaltation. To Timothy, Paul details just a few distinctive qualities, which separates Him from all else and also why He is to be first. Prayer Warriors, God is the King of the universe; as to His being, He is eternal! Furthermore, He is immortal and invisible. He cannot be seen or worshiped as a tangible form. He must be seen and worshiped through the "eyes of faith," and He is the only God there is; i.e., He is the only One of His kind. There is nothing, absolutely nothing, in the heavens or on the earth, comparable to the character, nature, or power of God the Almighty. He, He alone, is the Omnipotent One. David said,

"My eyes are ever toward the Lord, for He shall pluck my feet out of the net" (Psalm 25:15).
"Unto You I lift up my eyes, O You, who dwell in the heavens" (Psalm 121:1, TLB).

No wonder David was a man after God's own heart; his eyes were heavenward. His heart and soul looked to the hills of God's glory. For there he knew help was available, and prayer provided his heavenly view.

In like manner, Paul, the apostle, recognized God as the Invincible One and full of glory, the Almighty God, El Shaddai; words of honor and praise were to be heaped upon Him in abundance and forever! Paul and Silas have been arrested and are in the Philippian jail. They are innocent of any wrongdoings. What do we find them doing? What is the attitude of their spirit? It's the midnight hour and the other prisoners hear them praying and singing hymns to the Lord. In fact, they are in the spirit of worship. (Read Acts 16:25.) They considered prayer and worship the most important use of their time. They are not seen attempting to get some rest or fretting about how wrongly they had been treated or questioning God that He had failed them. Prayer and worship is the very character of their lives.

How is this spirit of worship, this "eye of faith," to become the spiritual, mental aspirations of us slow, limited, and wandering sheep of Jesus Christ? The answer is found in the admonition of Psalm 105:4: *"Seek the Lord and His strength; Seek His face evermore!"* For both Paul and David, the circumstance was not the issue. Their "eyes" saw the Lord, His strength, and His companionship. God, open the eyes of Your Church to see You, the Eternal, Almighty God!

There are two major priorities if one ever expects God to be first at the beginning of each new day and to see and witness the power and presence of Him who is omnipotent, omnipresent, and omniscient. There must be a time of devotion centered on reading the Holy Book. Reading the Bible is a time for listening; i.e., allowing God to speak and direct you. Next, as I continue to emphasize, seek His face through prayer, talking to Him. The word **seek** means to search, to inquire. Spending time in the closet of prayer is the opportunity to seek and ask for His strength, presence, power, and glory to abide with you. It also is a time to ask God for specific directions as you travel up and down the hills confronting you during the day. As toothpaste and brush, soap and water are to wash and cleanse us during the morning hours, The Word of God and prayer will cleanse you spiritually and prepare you for being God's testimony and enable you to go forth redeemed, cleansed, and robed in God's gracious strength and holy power for the day.

## SEEK THE COUNSEL OF GOD FIRST

One definition of the word **counsel** is that of seeking the advice, direction, or instructions from another person. Contrary to the thinking of our flesh and our human will, we are only weak, limited, and finite people. Thus if we are depending upon fleshly counsel to determine proper instructions for life, then total failure will be the results. Our rational, reasoning powers are totally inadequate to lead us aright. We need wisdom and discernment which we within ourselves are incapable of determining. The responsibilities of life and our walk with the One who has saved us are of such consequence that we simply cannot rely on the ingenuity of self-determination. We stand desperately in need of eternal wisdom that only God can provide. The most important preparation for the day is the help and guidance of God Himself through the leadership of His Holy Spirit. God sought the ear of David, to make him aware that it was He who would teach, direct, and guide him.

> "I will instruct you and teach you in the way you should go; I will guide you with My eye" (Psalm 32:8).

We need to remember that God's holy expression, His holy eyes are centered on us even as we are encouraged to focus our eyes on Him. God's eyes are centered upon us, but the question is, on what do we center our eyes? Moses, like Paul and David, realized that for him to be in God's will and accomplish His purpose in his life, then he must receive and listen to "the teaching" which comes from the very heart of God. Moses said to His Lord:

"If you are pleased with me, teach me your ways so I may know you and continue to find favor with you" (Exodus 33:13, NIV).

He knew that he was not capable of teaching God; God Himself was the Master Teacher. "Teach me your ways [why?] so I may know you. . . ."

Oh, for us Prayer Warriors to possess the spiritual mindset as those patriarchs of Scripture. They knew that for God to lead and instruct them, they must know His will for them. (Notice the word **knew**; remove the **"w,"** replace it with the letter **"e,"** and the word becomes **"knee."**) For them to know the counseling of the Lord, the method was on their knees before God. The Apostle Paul said to the Ephesian Church:

"For this reason I bow my knees to the Father of our Lord Jesus Christ" (Ephesians 3:14).

For God to lead, guide, instruct, and counsel us, there must be the sensitive ear tuned in to His Word and a desire to call on His name. Bow the knee, raise the eye heavenward, and wait. God will answer.

Referring to David again, we see that he had come to the understanding that it was God with whom he should converse first.

He should look for His direction first before undertaking any endeavor against his enemies. He had become a captain over four hundred fighting men. He had fled to the refuge of the cave of Adullam. What was he to do? How were he and his men to be rescued from possible slaughter? First he goes to Mizpah of Moab to converse with the king. There he made arrangement for the protection of his family; but what is really significant is what he said to the king of Moab.

> *"Please let my father and mother come here with you, till I know what God will do for me"* (1 Samuel 22: 3)

David's confidence was not focused on his own fighting abilities or that of his four hundred warriors. He wanted to know God's perspective. How was God viewing the situation? He knew he could trust the words and counsel of his God.

In 1 Samuel chapter 23, David is again faced with decision making. The Philistines are fighting against the city of Keilah. David is informed of the seriousness of the battle (v. 1), *"they [Philistines] are robbing the threshing floors."* What should he do, if anything? I am fearful that our mindset would be: "get going, enter into the battle, solve and defeat the conflict." We have a strong tendency to believe that the answer is to be found within self. Again, observe David's attitude.

> *"Therefore David inquired of the Lord, saying, Shall I go and attack these Philistines?"* (v. 2).

Serious-minded Prayer Warriors, do not take your Christian experience, your immortal God, or your own daily life for granted nor possess a nonchalant attitude. David realized the place of serious prayer in his life. The counsel of God was a prerequisite before striking out to get things done. David's question was, like the Apostle Paul's, "What do You want me to do?" How often he looked to God for counsel:

> *"But I call to God, and the Lord saves me. Evening, morning and noon I cry out in distress, and he hears my voice"* (Psalm 55:16-17, NIV).

How different the Biblical narrative of Eve and the deceitful serpent would have been if she had only remembered to go to the

Lord and sought His instructions. God had already given the warning, and it is best not to ignore what God says!

> *"And the Lord God commanded the man, 'You are free to eat from any tree in the garden; but you must not eat from the tree of the knowledge of good and evil, for when you eat of it you will surely die'"* (Genesis 2:16-17, NIV)

Oh! If only Eve had possessed the watchful eye of David. Evening, morning and noon he sought God's counsel and presence. Eve kept feeding on and looking intently at the temptation; and it brought about her downfall. She lost her innocence, her purity, and fellowship with her God. (See Genesis chapter 3.)

Prayer Warriors, let the chorus of the hymn "I Need Thee Every Hour" be your prayer activity as you prepare for the day.

> *"I need Thee, O I need thee; Ev'ry hour I need Thee! O bless me now, my Saviour. I come to Thee!"*

God is in His throne room waiting for His children to enter His presence, seek His face, and listen to His counsel as he speaks through His Word and Holy Spirit. Remember prayer and the Word are your spiritual weapons to give you victory for the day! Seek His holy face, listen to His counsel, and get His instructions for the day, for He has definite plans for you. The Lord said these words to the children of Israel even while they were in the Babylonian captivity:

> *"For I know the plans that I have for you, declares the Lord, plans for welfare and not for calamity to give you a future and a hope"* ( Jeremiah 29:11, NASB).

I know God has plans, good plans for His Church, plans of victory for His people. Yet you and I, the Church, have a serious responsibility. To know what His plans are the Church must awaken to His counsel. That means go and keep going to His throne! When the Church possesses the keen spiritual eye as a Moses, then the impossible becomes possible. The task, the challenge was too great for him. He did not have the intellectual fortitude to lead and guide the children of Israel. God was his source of knowledge. Moses needed the "spiritual map" which was in the mind of God Himself.

*"Now therefore, I pray, if I have found grace in Your sight, show me now*

*Your way*" (Exodus 33:13).

And the only way we can know God's way for us and for Him to show us His way is go to the "prayer closet" and through prayer and the Holy Spirit receive what God has to share and the instructions He desires to give. Amen!

# PART TWO

# THE HELPLESSNESS OF JESUS CHRIST, GOD'S HOLY SON

*"Most assuredly, I say to you, the Son can do nothing of Himself . . ." (John 5:19a).*

*(As Jesus acknowledged His helplessness in the flesh, how much more helpless must we be in our FLESH!)*

# Chapter 7
## *Jesus Christ, a Man of Humility*

The word **humility** is not a popular word in modern society. From my readings, I have learned that the great philosophers of ancient Greece did not find the character of humility a recommended garment to wear. To them it meant human weakness, and inadequacy, lack of strength and power; humility was an attire of unworthiness. Therefore, they were unsympathetic to anyone who displayed any action or conduct that could be interpreted or understood as being humble. To ancient Greeks, humility meant, not a man, only a weakling.

Even during this age of culture and refinement, and because of failure to understand what constitutes genuine character, there is still widespread ignorance of any meaningful attribute associated with this word **humility**. I dare say that even among most Church circles of today, the connotation of this word, like the Greek philosophers of old, means weakness, failure to perform, and being extremely lifeless. One must, therefore, target his search for a truthful answer and explanation of definition. One must look beyond the intellectual blindness of the worldly pagan's definition and allow the Person, Jesus Christ, to be your Guide of understanding. It is in Him, His human trait, not the glory and position in heaven He possessed, that teaches the world the precise meaning and truth of humility.

### THE HUMILITY OF JESUS CHRIST

The Apostle Paul was not one of the shepherds who heard the host of angels singing the glorious hymn of the birth of the Christ Child and visited Him in the manger at Bethlehem. Neither is there any Biblical reference that Paul was ever in Jesus' company as he grew from childhood to manhood. In fact, Paul, being the radical Pharisee that he was, understood Jesus to be simply a religious, pagan deceiver, a threat to the Hebrew faith, and thus these religious fanatics and followers of Jesus Christ must be stamped out. All traces of any Christian influence must be blotted out.

However, as Paul dogged his way toward Damascus, Syria for the purpose of capturing and killing those who professed Jesus as the

Messiah and their Saviour, he had a life-changing experience that revolutionized his total mission for all of life. For it was on this dusty road that he heard the piercing, penetrating voice of the very One he had been persecuting, and also he witnessed the glow of the heavenly light of Jesus Christ. In Acts 26:19 Paul calls it the "heavenly vision" when he testified before King Agrippa. He was changed by the power of Jesus Christ; and through the experience of his new birth and the fellowship he was now witnessing in Christ he came to an understanding of Jesus' humility. Realizing that a humble spirit is an essential wardrobe for the Christian Church, Paul wrote the following words to the Philippian Church:

> *"Let this same attitude and purpose and* [humble] *mind be in you which was in Christ Jesus: [Let Him be your example in humility.]"* (Philippians 2:5, AMP).

Paul came to a spiritual understanding of Christ's character of humility which too often is absolutely foreign to our humanistic mind. I believe that as Paul reflected on the sacred scene of the supernatural birth of God's only Son into this chaotic world, he knew and realized that the Bethlehem event was one of intense lowliness and must be taught and shared with others.

To me, in the past and even now the present, there hasn't been much preaching or emphasis centered on Christ's **self-denial,** and that His life and death are the very foundation of humility—the loss of self for others. As we study the scenes of Jesus' self-denial, it is then we really learn what humbleness is all about, for it is the spirit of Jesus Christ who must be our Example. That was Paul's conviction also. That is why, I believe, he wrote Philippians 2:5.

> *"Your attitude should be the kind that was shown us by Jesus Christ, who though he was God, did not demand and cling to his rights as God, but laid aside his mighty power and glory, taking the disguise of a slave and becoming like men. And he humbled himself even further, going so far as actually to die a criminal's death on a cross"* (Philippians 2:5-8, TLB).

Paul's conviction was to know Jesus Christ, to understand His surrender to the apparel of humanity; then one can appreciate and understand the true meaning of humility. In Paul's mind the best way to drive the point home to the Philippian Church is to declare Jesus' attitude toward His Deity.

The Apostle Paul was keenly aware that for Jesus to be born an infant and be placed in a manger, He had actually accepted the limitation associated with humanity. The glory He possessed in eternity was veiled in the garment of His becoming human. The Greek word used to declare Jesus' humble birth is *kenosis*, which means "emptying."

Wanting the Church at Philippi to come to a clear comprehension of what it meant for Christ, God's Anointed, to be born in this world of time and space, Paul digs deeply into the sacrifice Jesus had made. Paul wanted the Church to realize that Jesus was willing to forfeit the glory of heaven. Through His humble birth, physical life and abuse, His sufferings here on earth and ultimately the barbarity of the cross, Jesus' meekness was revealed. Paul's statement to the Church is that

*"Christ was humble. He obeyed God and even died on a cross"* (Philippians 2:8, CEV).

Paul's whole heartbeat is for the Church to grasp and understand the price both God and His Son Jesus Christ paid for their salvation. He was God; He had all the rights and majesty of heaven. Yet He did not tenaciously cling to His divine rights. Jesus was willing to become *"a bondservant . . . coming* [into the world] *in the likeness of men"* (see Philippians 2:7). Ironically, it was His becoming a man that enabled Jesus to bring glory to His Father. Read prayerfully and reverently this brief portion of His Priestly Prayer to His Father.

> *"I brought glory to you here on earth by doing everything you told me to do. And now, Father, bring me into the glory we shared before the world began"* (John 17:4-5, NLT).

This prayerful request of Jesus lifts our hearts from the dreadful scene of the cross, the enduring pain of God's Son, to His divine and holy position and relationship He had with His Father even before He spoke the world into existence. *"Father, bring me into the glory we shared before the world began."* Here Jesus is looking beyond the cross to that glorious exaltation of being one with His Father in the realm of eternal glory.

Prayer Warriors, to have a deeper and appreciative attitude toward God's love for us and of His Son's life here on earth, we must experience His *"kenosis."* We all need to admit our blurred spiritual vision and accept a serious, resounding rebuke of our failure to regard the depth of Christ's earthly humiliation. Before His submissive birth into this sinful, ungodly world to die for the sins of mankind, He bathed in the pure, radiant waters of His Father's love and presence.

Paul is urging his Christian readers to realize that for their lives to count for God, for there to be "salt" in their testimony, and for God to hear and answer their prayers, they must become sober and serious about living the Christian life. The Christian life is one of humility, meaning *self-denial*. To come to a definite realization what it means to be a sacrificial Christian, Paul says to the Church (and to us), "Look to Jesus, the Son of God; let Him be your Example." That means focusing on Christ's spirit and attitude, for He is the total essence of humility, that of losing sight of self so that others may live. As the Lord Jesus Christ was willing to lay aside and not cling to His heavenly rights and all its privileges, we too must seek through prayer and commitment to possess that holy mindset.

> "He [God] gave up, not just His glory to become man, but His own life—the just for the unjust, the deserving for the undeserving. His initiative broke the barrier."[1]

## HUMILITY A LOFTY POSITION

The first beatitude Jesus taught His disciples was the attribute of lowliness or humbleness.

> *"Humble men are very fortunate!"* he told them, *"for the Kingdom of Heaven is given to them."* (Matthew 5:2, TLB).

This beatitude describes the soul of the inner man and Christ's promise to bless and be with him, and of the Christian's future assurance. A humble posture before Christ and others, He will not ignore.

> *"For thus says the high and lofty One – He Who inhabits eternity, Whose name is Holy: I dwell in the high and holy place, but with him also who is of a thoroughly penitent and humble spirit, to revive the spirit of the humble and to revive the heart of the thoroughly penitent [bruised with sorrow for sin]"* (Isaiah 57:15, AMP).

The breath of the Lord refreshes the humble and graciously dwells within them, for this posture of the inner man acknowledges his total unworthiness. In His power God revives and gives spiritual life and assurance to those of a contrite spirit. His compassion for righteousness and holy conduct that will exalt His majestic name moves the Eternal, Holy One of Israel to notice intensely those of a contrite and humble spirit.

> *"This is what the Lord says: "Heaven is my throne and the earth is my footstool. This is the one I esteem; he who is humble and contrite in spirit, and trembles at my word"* (Isaiah 66:1a, 2b, NIV).

Listen to me, dear serious-minded Prayer Warriors. If we want and expect God to hear and answer prayer then we must assume the posture of humility. In God's sight it is a lofty disposition, for He does not and will not ignore a humble heart.

> *The Lord is near to those who have a broken heart, and saves those such as have a contrite spirit"* (Psalm 34:18)

Before closing this portion of the necessary spirit of humility in the life of a serious-minded pray-er, we must not omit Jesus' specific parable that teaches the contrast between **humility** and **pride**. Luke 18:9-14 records the attitude of two men. Both had gone to the temple to worship. (Incidentally, worship is to be one's motivation for attending Church.) One of the worshippers was clothed in an elegant garment of pride. He possessed an exalted evaluation of himself. He was a person of position and influence; he was a religious leader in the community, a Pharisee. He felt he had much to boast about and even made it known to God Himself. Verses 11 and 12 reveal his self-righteous disposition.

> *"The proud Pharisee stood by himself and prayed this prayer: "I thank you, God, that I am not a sinner like everyone else, especially like that tax collector over there! For I never cheat, I don't sin, I don't commit adultery, I fast twice a week, and I give you a tenth of my income"* (NLT).

It is obvious that this Pharisee does not see himself as God sees him. Furthermore, he doesn't really pray to God; he is simply gloating to himself over his self-righteous state and contrasting himself with those who have a reputation of cheating others, a publican, for example. Continuing to read his vain, empty prayer, he boasts of his goodness, not as the holy God sees him, but simply as he sees and evaluates himself. Prayer Warriors, the content of such praying will cause God Himself to regurgitate. Self-pride is the opposite of humility, and this Pharisee is drowning in it. He is so full of self-righteousness that there is no room for God. His prayer is a mockery to the sacredness of prayer. "The pride and arrogance of man are evil in God's sight, because there's nothing man can do without God's strength and might. We are never so empty as when we are full of self"[2]

Now let us consider the attitude and spirit of the tax collector. Like the Pharisee, he too went to the holy temple, the place of prayer. (Oh! for the sanctuary in our communities once again to become the place of prayer!) Again, like the Pharisee, he too prayed. However, his posture is evidence of his condemnation and an acknowledgment of his shame. Before his God, he knows he is guilty and deserves no mercy. He knows he is a sinner and *"fall[s] short of the glory of God"* (Romans 3:23).

> *"But the corrupt tax collector stood at a distance and dared not even lift his eyes to heaven as he prayed, but beat upon his chest in sorrow, exclaiming, 'God, be merciful to me, a sinner'"* (Luke 18:13, TLB).

Prayer that pleases and will find favor with God comes from an obedient, humble heart. Jesus warns against self-exaltation, but He promises reward to the humble.

> *"for everyone who exalts himself will be humbled, and he who humbles himself will be exalted"* (Luke 18:14b).

Thus, Prayer Warrior, how serious are you about prayer, about your prayer being heard and answered? Be clothed in the posture of humility, lose sight of self, and hunger and thirst for God's righteousness. Let the life and admonition of Jesus Christ be your guide. As He laid aside His heavenly glory for man's salvation, lay self aside, flee from selfish desires, and allow Jesus to be your blessing. John the Baptist realized the proper place; he longed for Jesus to be glorified and exalted for he said:

"*He [Jesus] must increase, but I must **decrease** [emphasis mine]*" (John 4:30).

---

***Pride is one of the Church's greatest enemies to prayer.***

---

Being humble may not be popular in the world, but it is a mode of life that God smiles upon. Pride is one of the Church's greatest enemies to prayer, for it blocks the avenue to God's presence and throne. The attitude and spirit of humbleness, which God desires for His child is that of complete surrender of one's **will**! That is exactly what Jesus did in the experience of becoming man, becoming human, knowing even before the foundation of the world that for Him to become man demanded His will to be totally surrendered, yielded to His Father's will. Thus,

"*...Being found in appearance as a man, He humbled* [surrendered] *Himself and became obedient to the point of death, even death on the cross*" (Philippians 2:8).

As Christ humbled Himself to the will of His Father, it is essential for us Prayer Warriors, in like manner, to surrender our will to God's holy will and direction for our lives. When we witness the experience of humility, which enables us to die to self and our self-will, we are in the position for the Master to hear and answer our prayers. The Father sees that we are **serious-minded Prayer Warriors!**

## NOTES

[1]Tim Stafford's Men's Devotional Bible Calendar, copyright, 1993, Dec. 26.
[2]*Our Daily Bread*, Sept.-Nov., 1995, Nov. 27.

# Chapter 8
## *Jesus Christ, the Man of Helplessness*

As we read Philippians 2:5-8, we can accept the fact that Jesus Christ, the Son of the eternal, holy God, took upon Himself *"the form of a bondservant, and became a human being here on earth."* Furthermore, we can accept and believe that He, Jesus, *"humbled Himself even further, going so far as actually to die a criminal's death on a cross"* (verse 8, TLB). However, to admit that He was **helpless** in any way while traveling the road of humility, that is a totally different matter altogether. Is it not blasphemy to make such a bold statement that Jesus, as a man, clothed with human flesh, was indeed helpless? That assertion must be proved from the evidence of Scripture before it can ever be acknowledged or accepted as being true. After all, even in the flesh, Jesus was still God's Son. Moreover, the Scripture explicitly affirms that Jesus and God are One (see John 17:2, 21).

> *Do you not believe that I am **in** (emphasis mine) the Father and that the Father is **in** (emphasis mine) Me? What I am telling you I do not say on My own authority and of my own accord, but the Father who lives in Me and the works—the miracles, His own deeds of power (John 14:10, AMP).*

Jesus does not say that He and His Father have similar characteristics or that He is very much like His Father. Very emphatically Jesus states: *"I and My Father are one."* In John 10, four times Jesus emphasizes the fact that He is in the Father and the Father is in Him. Thus, to even infer that Jesus here on earth was helpless, if not blasphemy, is a rash, bold statement.

### UNDERSTANDING JESUS' HELPLESSNESS

O. Hallesby says, **"Prayer and helplessness are inseparable. Only he who is helpless can truly pray."**[1]

In our modern world of independence and self-confidence, this word **helplessness**, like humility, has a strong negative connotation. To the contemporary mind, this word means lack of ability, inadequacy, not able to do or accomplish; and the secular world associates it as being destitute, feeble, incompetent. Assuming that these definitions portray accurately this word helplessness, then why would one dare to venture the thought that Jesus on earth was helpless? One must read The Book to understand clearly helplessness at its best. Its true meaning can not be found in the rough fabric of this world system. Again, just as Jesus portrays the real meaning and character of humility, He presents an accurate portrayal of being helpless and of the strength and power that are also available.

## *JESUS' AWESOME TASK*

The word **task** implies an assignment, a grave and serious responsibility. As this word relates to Jesus Christ, it refers to the responsibility He assumed here on earth. The prophet Isaiah declares the role of Christ's burden and yet His glory as God's Son in this world of sin.

> *"And the government will be upon his shoulder. And His name will be called Wonderful, Counselor, Mighty God, Everlasting Father, Prince of Peace"* (Isaiah 9:6b).

Isaiah also writes of the unique power that would enable Him to accomplish His awesome task, the Holy Spirit.

> *"The Spirit of the Lord God is upon Me, because the Lord has anointed Me to preach good tidings to the poor; He has sent Me to heal the brokenhearted, to proclaim liberty to the captives, and the opening of the prison to those who are bound. . . . The planting of the Lord, that He may be glorified"* (Isaiah 61:1, 3b)

In fact, the whole chapter of Isaiah sixty-one centers on the good news of salvation which God's Son was to provide for the world during Christ's life in the Hebrew world of Palestine.

If Jesus is to accomplish this significant role in this world of chaos, then He must first conquer and defeat His archenemy, and ours also—**satan!** 1 John 3:8b clearly denotes the conflict between Jesus and the works of the devil:

*"For this purpose the Son of God was manifested, that He might destroy the works of the devil"*

Furthermore, Jesus must constantly remember His Father's will for Him. In fact, it is because of His Father's will that Jesus came forth wearing the garment of humanity in the first place. Speaking to His disciples Jesus said,

*"My food is to do the will of Him who sent Me, and to finish His work"* (John 4:34; see John 6:38).

Because Jesus had humbled Himself in His willingness to become man, He was totally dependent upon His heavenly Father and the strength from Him. Jesus was keenly and acutely aware of His awesome task, and that He lacked human ability to fulfill it.

### What an enormous responsibility!

What an enormous responsibility! That is, to attempt what His Father had sent Him into the world to do, be the Saviour of the world and destroy the enemy of the world, satan himself! The question may very well be asked: "How can He do it? Better still, is He even able to do it? What will ever strengthen Him as He encounters such monstrous odds that will work strongly against Him? After all, Jesus is, like all of us, clothed in human flesh." Jesus knew the means by which His strength would come. It was His Father God and the Holy Spirit who would enable Him to shoulder the responsibility as a world conqueror, destroy the works of the devil, fulfill His Father's purpose, and ultimately be the Saviour of the world.

I do want to make it very clear that I do not minimize the Deity of Jesus Christ. He is the God-Man in the flesh. But we must remember that when He entered into the affairs of the human race, He emptied Himself of the glorious state He enjoyed in the portals of heaven with His Father. He declared His helplessness through these holy words.

*"So Jesus answered them by saying, 'I assure you, most solemnly I tell you, the Son is able to do nothing of Himself (of His own accord); but He is able to do only what He sees the Father doing,'"* (John 5:19, AMP). (See John 5:30; 8:28).

## THE ANSWER TO JESUS' HELPLESSNESS

God, who had chosen His only Son to accomplish a work that would deliver mankind from sin and the treacherous clutches of satan himself, and even more gloriously be the Saviour of the world, called His Son to be "the suffering Servant"! Even at an early age, Jesus had some insight as to His God-called purpose. At the tender age of twelve, Jesus declared to His parents, Mary and Joseph, their lack of understanding. Awakening their minds to His purpose in life,

> *"He said to them, "Why did you seek Me? Did you not know that I must be about My Father's business?"* (Luke 2:49).

It is obvious even to the casual Bible reader that Jesus was serious and felt the urgency of His mission to and in the world. He was determined to allow absolutely nothing to distract Him or preclude His fulfilling His divine call. He knew that He was in the world for a precise reason. His Holy Father had sent Him!

> *"And this is the will of Him who sent Me, that everyone who sees the Son and believes in Him may have everlasting life..."* (John 6:40).

The following words of Jesus to His disciples establish the fact that the work that the Father had designated Him to do was paramount.

> *"We must work the works of Him Who sent Me, and be busy with his business while it is daylight; night is coming on when no man can work"* (John 9:4, AMP).

As the title of this chapter alleges "Jesus Christ—The Man of Helplessness," in what way is there any evidence that Jesus was helpless or that He ever needed any kind of support to enable Him to do what His Father had sent Him into the world to effect?

## JESUS' TWO FOUNDATIONAL PILLARS

As we read the Word, we become aware that Jesus had two foundational pillars that supported Him strongly for the completion of the serious work God His Father had summoned Him to do. The first one is the **Paraclete, the Holy Spirit.** Isaiah 61:1 states very clearly the strength and power that was to undergird Jesus.

> "The Spirit of the Lord God is upon Me, because the Lord has **anointed** (emphasis mine) Me to preach good tidings to the poor; . . ."

To me this word **anointed** is the key word in the verse. It sheds light on Jesus' unique authority. It means to authorize, or set apart a person for a particular work or service. Jesus was totally dependent upon this holy anointing if He were to preach "good tidings" and glorify His Father on earth. This anointing was through Him the Paraclete. This word is a transliteration of the Greek word *parakletos*, which means "one who speaks in favor of, as an intercessor, advocate, or legal assistant."[2]

When Jesus entered this troubled, sin-cursed world, an infant child born in a manger, it was through the power of the Paraclete, the Holy Spirit Himself.

> "Then the angel said to her [Mary], The Holy Spirit will come upon you, and the power of the Most High will overshadow you (as a shining cloud); and so the holy (pure, sinless) Thing (offspring) which shall be born of you, will be called the Son of God" (Luke 1:35, AMP)

> "For with God nothing is ever impossible, and no word from God shall be without power or impossible of fulfillment" (Luke 1:37, AMP).

From the very beginning of His inception, His unique birth, it was through the power and ability of the Holy Spirit; and all through His earthly life there was the Paraclete accompanying Him. When Jesus entered into His public ministry, He submitted to the rite of baptism. John's Gospel doesn't write about the baptism of Jesus itself. He does, however, refer to the presence of the Holy Spirit descending upon Jesus like a dove.

> "And John [the Baptist] bore witness. saying, "I saw the Spirit descending from heaven like a dove and He remained upon Him" (John 1:32).

When Jesus faces off with the devil in the wilderness (desert). who leads Him? It is no other than the **Paraclete** (see Matthew 4:1-

11). Next we see Jesus returning to Galilee, but He does not travel alone.

*Then Jesus returned in the power of the Spirit to Galilee . . . (Luke 4:14).*

## REMEMBER WE TOO ARE HELPLESS

One of the greatest misconceptions of the Church is its trusting in its own sufficiency. So often the pastor, staff, and even many "lay folk" feel that if the right program can be found, the right strategy established (some leaders would even use the word gimmick; that is, a tricky device; a clever new stratagem), they will be successful. The work of the Lord is not designed for gimmicks or clever schemes. The birth-pains of the Lord's work is born through agonizing prayer and the power of the Holy Spirit. The great missionary of the New Testament, the Apostle Paul, realized that to accomplish the work of the Lord demanded much more than his human wisdom. He said,

*"Not that we are sufficient of ourselves to think of anything as being from ourselves, but our **sufficiency** [emphasis mine] is from God"* (2 Corinthians 3:5).

Oh, Prayer Warriors, let us all awaken to the fact that we too are totally helpless. Even as Paul acknowledged his depend ence upon his God, it is time that we confess that we are without spiritual strength. If the Holy Spirit is absent in our lives and the life and ministry of the Church, the purpose of its existence is of no avail. Again referring to the Apostle Paul, he wrote to the Philippian Church of the two pillars, prayer and the Holy Spirit!

*"For I know that this will turn out for my deliverance through your prayer and the supply of the Spirit of Jesus Christ"* (Philippians 1:19).

The Old Testament prophet, Zechariah, states in detail that the work of the Lord is dependent, not on self-ability or initiative, but on the ministry of the Holy Spirit.

*"This is the word of the Lord to Zerubbabel: 'Not by might nor by power, but by my Spirit,' says the Lord Almighty"* (Zechariah 4:6, NIV).

Just as Jesus and Paul knew their helplessness to fulfill the

Father's will without the pillar, the Paraclete, who was both their Strengthener and Companion, we too are just as helpless. Before Jesus' ascension to His Father, He warned the apostles that to do and accomplish God's will, they had no strength without the holy anointing of the Holy Spirit. His words to them are very succinct.

> *"But you will receive power when the Holy Spirit comes on you . . ."* (Acts 1:8, NIV).

Yes, Jesus rested His total ministry on two pillars, the one being the Paraclete, the power and holy unction of the Holy Spirit. (Chapter nine identifies the second pillar that Jesus depended upon to enable Him to meet the demand toward man's salvation).

Dressed in the clothing of humanity, Jesus lacked spiritual power to accomplish His Father's will; but as He looked to, depended on, and sought the power of the Holy Spirit, this glorious Pillar supported His every footstep. Prayer Warriors, may that same Pillar be your foundational stone also.

## NOTES

[1] O Hallesby, *Prayer, A World Famous Classic*, Augsburg Publishing House, Minneapolis, Mn., Copyright 1931, Copyright renewed 1959, 1975 Pocket Paperback Edit. (p. 17).

[2] *Nelson's Illustrated Bible Dictionary*, Carmel, New York, General Edit. Herbert Lockyer, Sr. (p. 800).

# Chapter 9
## *Prayer! — Jesus' Strong Pillar*

**Prayer** is the other strong pillar Jesus depended upon to enable Him to do and complete the ministry His Father had commissioned Him. From the very beginning of Jesus' public ministry, prayer was His strong pillar. He appears not to have taken any forward step without first inquiring His Father's will through prayer. Knowing He must be obedient daily to His Father's desire, prayer was the spiritual pillar and foundation that supported Him. Using another analogy, prayer was the spiritual avenue He must travel, and He never lost sight of this divine road of communion which He had with His heavenly Father. Jesus is the prime example for each Prayer Warrior and for the effectiveness of the Christian Church. He knew the *need, power, and results* of prayer. Oh! May we allow God to awaken us to the need, power, and results of prayer in our own lives and ministry!

### JESUS' SPIRITUAL POWER THROUGH PRAYER

Jesus' baptismal experience, by John the Baptist in the River of Jordan, ushers Jesus into His public ministry. It is His announcement that He is now coming out of obscurity and making Himself known as the Son of God. This event in the life of Jesus is significant enough that it is recorded in the writings of the four gospels (Matthew 3:13-17; Mark 1:9-11; Luke 3:21, 22; John 1:31-34). Only Luke, though, records Jesus' praying while being baptized.

> "Now when all the people were baptized, and when Jesus also had been baptized, and **[while He was still] praying** [emphasis mine], the [visible] heaven was opened, And the Holy Spirit descended upon Him in bodily form, like a dove..." (Luke 3:21-22, AMP).

Observe this detailed information Luke shares with his readers. The Holy Spirit did not come upon Jesus as His pillar of guidance and strength simply because He was being baptized. It was while **He was praying,** being in communion with His Father, that the Holy Spirit made His appearance in the form of a dove and sat on Jesus' shoulder. My question is this: would the Holy Spirit have come to

Jesus if He had neglected to pray? The writer Luke makes it clear that it was while Jesus was praying that the Holy Spirit came upon Him. The radiant dove, the Holy Spirit Himself, was the pillar of strength that fortified Him to face His arch enemy, satan, endure the forty days of fasting, and defeat satan as he hurled his sly darts at Him. I believe, Prayer Warriors, in fact, I am convinced, that it was because Jesus adhered to prayer as His foundational base for His public ministry that the Holy Spirit moved upon the dramatic scene of Jesus' life.

## JESUS' PREPARATION TO MINISTER

The writer Mark in his gospel is noted for moving very rapidly as he surveys the life of Christ to his readers. It is interesting, though, to note his rather detailed sketch of how Jesus uses His time during one day of activities; but first he recapitulates Jesus' preparation for this enormous ministry. As I have taken time to record Jesus' busyness that is recorded in Mark chapter one, may you recognize that Jesus still *carved out* essential time for prayer.

Chapter one, verse one introduces Mark's readers to the Gospel. *"The beginning of the gospel of Jesus Christ, the Son of God."*

Verses two and three record the prophecy of John the Baptist and his purpose of preparing the way for the Lord Jesus. Verses four through seven relate John's baptismal service and his preaching *"a baptism of repentance for the remission of sins."* Verse eight is John's testimony that he baptizes with water, *"but he [Jesus] will baptize you with God's Holy Spirit!"* (TLB). It isn't until verse nine, however, that there is the introduction of Jesus actually on the scene and of His travel from Nazareth of Galilee to the River Jordan to be baptized by John the Baptist. Verses ten and eleven refer to Jesus' baptismal experience itself and the appearance of the Holy Spirit. Verses twelve and thirteen record Jesus' temptation experience, *"and the angels ministered to Him."*

## JESUS BEGINS A BUSY DAY OF ACTIVITIES (*vv.* 14-34).

I have numbered events in Jesus' busy ministry one through twelve. I want you to see just what occupied Jesus' time during His one day of ministry; and yet He **made time** to pray and commune with His Father. To Jesus, I don't believe anything else was more important. The pillar of prayer He could not afford to disregard! His effectiveness came through the Holy Spirit and prayer.

1. Verse 14 records John the Baptist being in prison and Jesus begins His ministry in Galilee. Let's walk with Him through this one day of activities.

> "*Jesus came to Galilee, preaching the gospel of the kingdom of God.*"

> "*Then Jesus returned in the power of the Spirit to Galilee, and news of Him went out through out all the surrounding region*" (Luke 4:14).

2. Verse 15 records Jesus' message: "*The time is fulfilled, and the kingdom of God is at hand* [has drawn near]. *Repent, and believe in the gospel.*"

This occasion of preaching the gospel, the Good News, and calling people to repentance demanded much of Jesus' time; but **time** is what Jesus used to declare the truth of the gospel.

## JESUS CALLS FOUR MEN TO DISCIPLESHIP

3. Verse 16—Now we see Jesus walking "*by the Sea of Galilee* [and] *He saw Simon and Andrew his brother casting a net into the sea, for they were fishermen.*"

4. Verse 17—Jesus' challenge to these common laborers: "*Follow Me, and I will make you become fishers of men.*" (See Matthew 4:19.)

5. Verse 19—"*And when He had gone a little farther from there, He saw James the son of Zebedee, and John his brother, who also were in the boat mending their nets.*"

6. Verse 20—records Jesus' calling them to become His disciples also.

My point of emphasis recording Jesus' activities is that after spending time preaching the new birth and calling people to repentance and urging them to believe the gospel, I would expect Him to be extremely tired. (As I visualize Jesus' active schedule, it tires me.) If I had committed myself to such an industrious agenda I would have been saying to myself, "I need a break; I have done enough for one day; I need the recliner." Not so with Jesus, though.

## JESUS TRAVELS TO CAPERNAUM

7. After preaching repentance and calling four disciples to walk with Him throughout His public ministry, verse 21 states Jesus' first

activity after entering Capernaum. Notice, He did not seek out a restaurant to meet any physical comfort or a Lazy Boy to rest His tired feet. Again, remember Jesus has been declaring the gospel of repentance; He has challenged four men to follow Him in discipleship. Also He has traveled to another city, Capernaum. Wouldn't your physical energy be depleted after engaging in that much activity? Not so with Jesus, however. It is the Sabbath *"and immediately on the Sabbath He entered the synagogue and taught."*

8. Verse 22—His listeners were amazed as they heard His message. *"And they were astonished at His teaching, for He taught as one having authority, and not as the scribes."*

## JESUS HEALS A MAN WITH AN UNCLEAN SPIRIT

9. Verse 23 informs us that one of the listeners in the synagogue had an unclean spirit. *"And he [the unclean spirit] cried out."*

10. Verses 24 and 25 relate Jesus' confrontation with the unclean spirit and His power to heal the man. *"But Jesus rebuked him, saying, 'Be quiet, and come out of him!'"*

11. Verse 27—Those in the synagogue, who witnessed the demonstration of Jesus' healing power, were amazed: *"Then they were all amazed, so that they questioned among themselves, saying, 'What is this? What new doctrine is this? For with authority He commands even the unclean spirits, and they obey Him.'"* This event causes *"His fame [to] spread throughout all the region around Galilee"* (See v. 28). Is it not time for Jesus to call it a day? Not so with Jesus, for there are others standing in need of His compassion and love.

## JESUS HEALS PETER'S MOTHER-IN-LAW

11. Verse 29 says: *"Now as soon as they had come out of the synagogue they entered the house of Simon and Andrew, with James and John."* Here, there are no crowds, only Jesus and His four disciples and, of course, Peter's mother-in-law. However, when Jesus enters the house, He sees that the woman of the house is ill. Because of a fever, she can't prepare any food for them. So rather than unwinding, kicking off His sandals, and calling it a day well spent, Jesus goes into action to meet the need of the hour.

12. Verse 30, *"But Simon's wife's mother lay sick with a fever, and they told Him about her at once."*

*How many of our burdens do we carry rather than sharing them with Jesus at once? Nothing is said in the Word that we are to "work" everything out ourselves.*

In fact, the Word encourages just the opposite.

*"Cast your burden [your work] on the Lord, and He shall sustain you; He shall never permit the righteous to be moved"* (Psalm 55:16).

At once, Jesus is made aware of her physical need. God's Word does teach us,

*"Be anxious for nothing, but in everything by prayer and supplication, with thanksgiving, let your requests be made known to God"* (Philippians 4:6).

(See Matthew 6:25—"Don't be a WORRIER!") When will we Christians awaken to the fact that Jesus is to be told **"at once"**?

13. Verse 31 tells us exactly how Jesus responded to her sickness: *"So He came and took her by the hand and lifted her up, and immediately the fever left her. And she served them."*

**Serious Question:** Would Jesus have healed Peter's mother-in-law if He had not been told **at once** by His disciples?

## NOW IT IS SUNSET

What do we normally do when the sun darkens behind the clouds and it is evening time? Get settled in a comfortable chair, read the newspaper, and watch TV. Well what about Jesus? Surely He is by now totally and completely exhausted; He has yielded Himself, His time, to a full day of ministering to the needs of others, including His healing ministry to Peter's mother-in-law. Yet it is a total different story in the life and ministry of Jesus. Never do we see Him thinking only of Himself and His own comfort. His life in the flesh is still lived for others. Night has settled in, but Jesus, who is the Son of Man, has only one thought, the needs of others.

14. Verses 32-34 speak clearly how Jesus spent His evening.
(v. 32) *"At evening, when the sun had set, they brought to Him all who were sick and those who were demon-possessed. (v. 33) And the whole city gathered at the door. (v. 34) Then He healed many who were sick with various diseases, and cast out many demons; and He did not allow the demons to speak, because they knew Him."*

## THE CLIMAX

I know it has been somewhat a tedious task to follow Jesus during this one day of serious ministry. Did you observe just how demanding His time was for the benefit of others? Certainly one would think that after such a day and evening of busyness, one full of intense giving, as Jesus had given of Himself for others, He would surely sleep in and probably omit an early "prayer time" with His Father. Surely it wouldn't hurt to miss this one time. Verse 35, to me, is the climax. It discloses to us just what Jesus considered to be most important to Him as He entered into a new day.

*"Now in the morning, having risen a long while before daylight, He went out and departed to a solitary place; and there He prayed."*

**Jesus never became too tired to pray; He did not neglect His morning devotions!**

---

*Prayer Warriors, don't neglect your prayer time! Prayer was not a burden to Jesus; it was His delight.*

---

The word **neglect** means **"to put off, to delay"** doing what may need to be done. I must admit that I do put some things off. For example, I put off at times mowing the yard. I enjoy driving past a house and viewing the flowers and a well-trimmed lawn. I, on the other hand, would much rather spend my time reading and studying than spending time working in the yard. I mow and trim simply because it needs to be done, not because I enjoy it. Also, I may neglect taking out the wastebasket. I may tell my wife that I will do it a little later, not now. I may have something else I consider more important to do. There may be many things we all may neglect or fail to do and there are no serious consequences. The neglect, the putting off, the delay of prayer, however, is extremely serious. It means time for prayer is not all that important to us; it means that prayer is not considered to be very vital to seek definite direction for the day. As Jesus entered into a brand new day, He knew that prayer was His essential pillar. It would sustain Him as He faced the immense challenge of the day. The Holy Spirit was His power for the day and prayer was His talking to His Father to receive specific guidance. Prayer Warriors that is the same way and the only way that we too may acquire the power to fulfill God's purpose within our own lives and the life of the Church. "God, help us" is my prayer! Jesus realized the significance of prayer in His own life. Before facing the formidable task each new day presented to Him, it was **prayer first!**

Psalm 34 teaches us the significance of prayer, time spent with Jehovah God: (v. 4) *"I sought the Lord, and He heard me, And delivered me from all my fears."* Would God have delivered if there had not been first the seeking; would God have heard if there had been the neglect of calling on Him?

Psalm 34:11 is an earnest admonition to prayer: *"Come, you children, listen to me; I will teach you the fear of the Lord."* However, for the Lord to teach us, there must be the going before Him. The Spirit of the Lord cannot teach us unless we **"listen,"** and allow Him to share with us His teachings and blessings.

Verse 15 is a great promise to those who do not neglect their time with God. *"The eyes of the Lord are on the righteous. And His ears are open to their cry."* Notwithstanding, God's ears, as such, must hear the cries of prayer before there can be an answer.

God considered David to be one after His own heart. Why? I believe David was convicted that **Prayer Time** was the most significant use of his time. He, like Jesus, refused to disregard this, priceless foundation called prayer!

"Dear God, be merciful to us as we are so prone to neglect what You desire most from us, communion with You in prayer!"

Andrew Murray challenges us with these words: "Take time to think of what a cry of need there is throughout the whole Church, and throughout all our mission fields. Let us realize that the only remedy to be found for inefficiency or impotence, to enable us to gain the victory over the powers of darkness, is in the manifested presence of our Lord in the midst of His hosts and in the power of His Spirit. Let us take time to think of the state of all the Churches throughout Christendom until we are brought deeper than ever to the conviction that nothing will avail except the supernatural, almighty intervention of our Lord Himself, to rouse His hosts for the great battle against evil. Can anyone conceive or suggest any other matter for prayer that can at all compete with this: for the power of God on the ministers of the gospel, and on all His people, to endue them with power from on high to make the gospel in very deed the power of God unto salvation?"[1]

Jesus knew He must have and depend on the pillar of prayer, as well as the Holy Spirit, for His ministry to be successful, and, Prayer Warriors, we too must have this same dynamic pillar!

## NOTES

[1] Andrew Murray, *The Secret of United Prayer*, "Prayer for All the Fullness of the Spirit," Copyright 1998, CLC Publications, pp. 60, 61.

# Chapter 10

## *Jesus' Prayer Life: Our Greatest Example*

As the apostles followed Jesus, listened to His teaching, and witnessed His powerful miracles, they asked Him many questions and even appealed to Him to do many things. To me, their petition, asking Him to teach them to pray, indicates their desire for a deeper insight and understanding of prayer.

> *Now it came to pass, as He was praying in a certain place* [Jesus had a prayer closet], *when He ceased, that one of His disciples said to Him, "Teach us to pray, as John taught His disciples"* (Luke 11:1).

Evidently these apostles sensed that Jesus possessed an affection toward God that they themselves did not have. E. M. Bounds says, "As they listened to Him praying, they felt very keenly their ignorance and deficiency in praying."[1] They must have remained there for a time listening to Jesus praying for it says, "when He ceased." (Jesus did not hurry through His prayer time with His Father.)

I believe that prayer was the most serious conviction in the heart of Jesus. He had a responsibility that involved all eternity, and He must have the two pillars mentioned in the previous chapter. Thus, He relied on communion with His Father for the essential guidance needed for each day.

### JESUS' MORNING DEVOTIONS

Again, as was pointed out in the previous chapter, Jesus did not neglect His "morning devotions." Morning devotions! That means seeking and seeing the face of God before seeing the face of the TV or that of the market place. Question: How do most of us, yes, "us," we Christians, prepare for the new day that is before us? We devote much time getting our bodies groomed. That is, we do all the physical essentials, bathing or showering, brushing our teeth, and, of course, selecting what to wear for the day. That is needful, but it has nothing to do with establishing strength, spiritual strength, or any ability to accomplish God's will in your life for the day. Most mornings I wash my face, brush my teeth, and then go to be with my Lord, spending time in His Word and entering into dialogue with Him in prayer. One morning, though, before meeting with my Lord in the "prayer closet," I shaved, brushed my teeth, and showered; I did all the necessary preparation which is considered proper toward physical grooming for the day. When I began, I checked the time and again when I had finished. I had spent 35 minutes getting myself tidied up for the day. The thought hit me: 35 minutes devoted to the physical, getting the body groomed, "dressed up" for the new day that was before it. As so much time is devoted to the external, how much time is devoted to getting the "inner man" ready for the challenges of the new day? One should certainly give time to the necessities of the body, but how much time are we willing and desiring to give to cleansing and purifying the inner man? Soap and water will eliminate all impurities of the physical, but *the Word and prayer* are the spiritual soap and water for the soul of man!

The heart of Jesus' ministry was the holy unction of the Holy Spirit who was to strengthen, energize, and supply Him for the task facing Him that day. Not trusting or relying on oratorical ability, He began the day early, having His morning devotions.

It is time, past time, for the Christian Church to awaken to its means of authority and power. Prayer, invoking the holy presence of the Holy Spirit, is the means of witnessing this powerful, dynamic authority. Jesus, knowing this principle of truth, knowing that prayer was His pillar that fortified Him, did not allow other "things" to so monopolize His time that He ignored the pillar of strength that prepared Him for service. Furthermore, Jesus, I believe, simply enjoyed these "closet experiences"; they were extended moments which enabled Him to spend time with His Father. Oh, for the Church to understand and view prayer as precious moments of entering into heaven's presence as Jesus did. Dear God, awaken the Church, God's redeemed ones, to begin each day with You before beginning it with anyone else!

## JESUS' EVENING DEVOTIONS

Mark chapter 6 gives us a brief sketch of Jesus' busy ministry during a day. Verses one through six speak of Jesus' opposition in Nazareth. On the Sabbath *"He began to teach in the synagogue. . . ."* However, His listeners resented Him and questioned His authority.

They saw Him only as Mary's son and having brothers and sisters (see vv. 2, 3). In fact, Jesus is amazed of the depth of their unbelief (see v. 6). Therefore, He left Nazareth and as verse 6b says, *"Then Jesus went out from village to village, teaching"* (NLT).

The following scene is of Jesus sending His apostles on their first missionary assignment (see vv. 7-12). He assured them of spiritual power and authority that would enable them to do remarkable miracles. Before continuing with Christ and His activities and of His apostles, though, Mark inserts the experience of John the Baptist being put in prison and the reason why and of his death (see vv. 14-29). In vv. 30-44 Mark again picks up Jesus' activities. He records the excitement of the apostles' tone as they relate to Jesus all they had done and taught (see v. 30).

Even Jesus felt the need for physical rest; thus He said to His apostles, *"Let's get away from the crowds and rest"* (v. 31a, NLT). However, such a multitude of people followed Him, they couldn't even find time to eat. Verse 32 informs us just how desperate Jesus was for some rest and quietness. *"They left by boat for a quieter spot"* (NLT), to get away from the crowd which still proved to be an impossibility. When they landed the boat, *"A vast crowd was there as he stepped from the boat . . ."* (v. 34, NLT). How does Jesus respond to this dilemma? He is tired and hungry; He feels the need to rest His weary body, but the people surrounding Him won't allow Him and the apostles any time for self. Moreover, He had a congregation of more than 5000 following after Him (see v. 44). Even though Jesus is tired and fatigued (may have been totally exhausted), His love and compassion for them came first. *"He had compassion on them because they were like sheep without a shepherd. So he taught them many things"* (see v. 34, NLT).

By now it is late in the evening and the apostles considered where they were. They requested Jesus to send the crowd to their various homes (see v. 36; Matthew 14:15; Luke 9:12). Jesus' thoughts were not centered upon His own discomfort or the apostles. He saw tired, exhausted followers as sheep without a shepherd (see Mark 6:34). Thus Jesus performed the miracle of feeding the 5000 plus wives and children with the menu being five loaves of bread and two fish, which was a small lunch belonging to a lad (see John 6:9).

Now, Prayer Warriors, wouldn't you be "dead tired" if you put in a long day as Jesus had? Wouldn't you want to "hit the sack" as soon as possible? Let's notice what Jesus did. Nothing is said about Jesus or his apostles eating or of His saying to His apostles, "Let's get to bed, for I am very weary having put in so many hours of service for others, and we have much to do tomorrow." He simply sends His apostles to Bethsaida in a boat and *"he sent the people home"* (see Mk. 6:45, NLT). Jesus wants quietness and to be alone. Why? He is to have His "evening devotions."

>*Afterwards he went up into the hills by himself to pray* (Mk. 6:46, NLT).

I imagine the content of Jesus' prayer to His Father contained words of praise and thankfulness for the evidence of the Holy Spirit and the companionship of His Father being with Him throughout the day and enabling Him to perform miracles and meeting the needs of the people, especially the feeding of the 5000. Charles Spurgeon states, relative to Jesus' early prayer time (which I call "His morning devotions"), "I delight to think of our Lord as praying before He did a great thing."[2] I definitely agree with him; I would only add that I delight to think that Jesus had His evening devotions to thank His Father for the "great things" achieved during the day, for miracles which exalted His heavenly Father.

Prayer Warriors, let us awaken out of our spiritual sleep and realize just how much we neglect both our morning and evening devotions. So many things, yes, even worthy things, absorb much of our time and hinder our devotions to our Lord Jesus. As busy as He was, Jesus still made it His priority to have both His morning and evening communion with His Father. God help us to awaken to what is really important!

### JESUS' DEVOTIONS BETWEEN MORNING AND EVENING

No one had ever come on the scene of life and affected it as Jesus had. He spoke with intense authority and even the demons bowed in fear of His command to be gone. When He said, *"Be quiet!"* . . . *"Come out of him!"* (see Mark 1:25), the only thing the evil spirit could do was come *"out of him* [[the man] *with a shriek"* (see Mark 1:26). Jesus was a man of miracles and dynamic power. Thus His popularity spread like "wild fire." It was extremely difficult for Jesus to find time to be alone. He did arise early for His "morning devotions" and at evening time when people thought about sleep for the night, He could steal away and have His "evening devotions" with His Father; but what was He to do during the day, for *"great multitudes came together to hear, and to be healed by Him of their infirmities"* (Luke 5:15)?

The Living Bible (Paraphrased) depicts Jesus' dominance and influence as though the uniqueness of His gospel, His healing ministry, and the power of His message intoxicated the people.

*"Now the report of his power spread even faster and vast crowds came to hear him preach and to be healed of their diseases"* (Luke 5:15).

It appears that Jesus was surrounded by a stampede of people from morning until late at night. Yet in the midst of His dynamic ministry, His seeing the multitude as sheep without a shepherd and having a heart full of compassion for them (see Matthew 9:35, 36), and, of course, the fervor of His popularity, Jesus never forgot His source of power and strength which enabled Him to do His Father's will. He still, even during the day, "carved out" those precious moments for prayer. He knew that He could not allow even His time-consuming ministry to rob Him of the fellowship He desired and actually craved in prayer to commune with His Father. Luke 5:16 relates just how important this comradeship between Father and Son was to Jesus.

*"So He Himself **often** [emphasis mine] withdrew into the wilderness and prayed."*

This word **often** means "many times." Hence, I believe that "many times" during the day Jesus, realizing His need for spiritual power to undergird Him and His pastoral care, would withdraw Himself from the press caused by the crowd and go to His prayer closet, for it was time for Holy Communion. Depicting Jesus in prayer, Charles Spurgeon says, "He kneels, He cries, He supplicates, He speaks with God, He prays."[3]

It seems that for Jesus to prepare Himself for the labor during the day, delivering His message of truth, that absolutely nothing could replace His prayer life. Jesus knew that the miracles He performed, even all the good He did for the poor and the "down-and-outers," were not the source of His spiritual strength. Prayer to Jesus was essential and there was no other avenue He could travel. There was no other pillar stable enough to support Him; it was **prayer** and the power of the **Holy Spirit** that held Him fast to preach, heal, and ultimately die for the world, to die for you and me. Indeed, it was **prayer** and the **Holy Spirit** that enabled Jesus to walk the path of total obedience of His Father.

Prayer Warriors, the life of the Christian faith and obedience to the will of our heavenly Father demand both the leadership of the Holy Spirit and a serious commitment to prayer. Jesus knew that for Him to please His Father, prayer was His most important pillar. **God help us and awaken us** out of our spiritual sleepiness and carnality. Prayer, serious-minded prayer, is the Church's most urgent need during these horrible days of ungodliness. Prayer Warriors, grasp both the privilege and seriousness of the pillar of prayer: "Our Master set an example for us. Remember how often He went to be *alone with God!* And there was a powerful purpose behind His command, *'when you pray, go into your room, close the door and pray'* (Matthew 6:6)."[4]

## NOTES

[1]*The Complete Works of E. M. Bounds on Prayer*, Baker Book House Company, Grand Rapids, MI, Copyright 1990, p. 249.
[2]Charles Spurgeon, *The Power of Christ's Prayer Life*, YWAM Publishing, Seattle, WA, p. 29.
[3]Ibid., p. 29.
[4]L. B. Cowman, *Streams in the Desert*, Zondervan Publishing House, Grand Rapids, Mi., Copyright 1925, 1953, 1965, and 1997, Feb. 27, p. 91.

# PART THREE

# THE SPIRITUAL APPLICATION OF PRAYER

*"You therefore, my son, be strong in the grace that is in Christ Jesus. And the things that you have learned from me among many witnesses, commit these to faithful men who will be able to teach others also" (1 Timothy 2:1-2).*

*"Then Jesus said, 'Come to me, all of you who are weary and carry a heavy burden, and I will give you rest. Take my yoke upon you. Let me teach you, because I am humble and gentle, and you will find rest for your souls'" (Matthew 11:28-29, NLT).*

# Chapter 11
## *Things Learned*

*"Let Me teach you"* Matthew 11:29 NLT. Indeed, that was Jesus' desire. He taught; it was up to His disciples to listen and learn. To learn! For a person to learn, to grasp, to understand means paying serious attention to what is being said and taught. It demands concentrating and focusing fully on the one who is teaching. Jesus taught through His life, conduct, priorities, miracles, and messages. In fact, His total ministry with His apostles was to teach them the truth of the Gospel that they may continue the message to the world.

The Apostle Paul wrote words that were very similar to the words of Jesus. To the Church at Philippi he wrote:

*"The things which you learned and received and heard and saw in me, these do, and the God of peace will be with you"* (Philippians 4:9).

Paul, like Jesus, is emphasizing the fact that he had been with them. They had learned, received, heard him, and had seen him do and accomplish through God's power. Now they were to apply, put into action what they had learned from him, and the peace of God will abide with them. In like manner, Jesus told His apostles to take His yoke upon them, pay attention to what He had taught them, and put it into action.

Webster's dictionary says that since Old English times, the word **learn** has always meant "to gain knowledge." Paul the Apostle had a clear understanding of this word **learn.** Having poured his heart out to the "babes in Christ" in Philippi, he urged them to keep foremost in their hearts what he had taught them. For example, Paul had shared with these early Christians what living and dying meant to him.

*"For to me, to live is Christ, and to die is gain"* (Philippians 1:21).

He had taught them that his only goal and purpose for life was for the glory of the One who had saved and changed him completely. To him, life meant Christ, his only purpose for living. His attitude toward death was also founded in the assurance of Jesus Christ. How he died was not the major issue; that is, whether his death was by failing health or by the sting of martyrdom. Because of his dynamic faith in his Jehovah God, and the power of prayer, life or death meant only one thing to him— means of exalting his Lord, and to die to him simply meant "gain." Paul had no horrible thoughts about the experience of death. It merely meant he was entering into the heavenly realm of God's glory. Yes, that is what Paul had taught this early Church. Also he had shared with them the genuine spirit of Jesus Christ. As he expounded in detail of Christ joining the human race and becoming a human being, Paul emphasized humbleness and he implored these infant Christians, in like manner, to be dressed in the garment of humility. Yes, that too was a significant message Paul had taught this young Church.

Warnings were also a crucial aspect of Paul's teaching. The word **warning** indicates the threat of impending dangers, and Paul knew that evil workers were lurking in and out of corners of opportunity seeking ways and means to twist the truth of the gospel. Paul's thriving thrust for the Philippian Church was for them to know the truth, walk and live in the truth of Jesus, and be clothed in the holy attire of humility that Jesus Himself had manifested. Definitely, Paul again, like Jesus Christ, taught prayer to this struggling Church. He exhorted them to live their Christian life in faith and to depend entirely on Christ. Don't allow anxiety, worry, or frustration, he admonished, to possess your hearts. **Be a Church of prayer, a Church of Prayer Warriors!** Paul taught:

> "Be anxious for nothing, but in everything by prayer and supplication, with thanksgiving, let your requests be known to God" (Philippians 4:6).

I like the wording of the Living Bible:

"Don't worry about anything; instead pray about everything. Tell God your needs and do not forget to thank Him for His answers."

These are just a few of the valuable lessons of truth Paul taught the Church, and he urged them:

> The things which you learned and received and heard and saw in me, these do, and the God of peace will be with you (Philippians 4:9).

In like manner, my burden of concern is that you, precious Prayer Warriors, will not simply read these chapters in this prayer book God has given to me, but that you will hear and follow the admonition of Jesus and Paul. Jesus said, *"Let me teach you."* Paul, in like manner, admonished the Church:

*"Keep putting into practice all you learned from me and heard from me and saw me doing, and the God of peace will be with you"* (Philippians 4:9, NLT).

Both Jesus and Paul are encouraging their listeners to make these vital teachings the CENTERPIECE of their Christian life! Then claim God's promise: *"and the God of peace will be with you."*

As you, Prayer Warriors, have read Part One, "The Privilege of Prayer," and Part Two, "The Prayer Life of Jesus Christ," what have you read that applies to your own "prayer life"? Have you been exposed to what you need to accept and implement in your own prayer life? Unless you have been challenged in the area of application, either this "prayer book," or "your reading," has missed the spiritual mark.

**Application** becomes a reality when there is the applying what has been heard and learned. Because of what Israel had seen—the commandments, statutes, and judgments they had been exposed to—they were to accept, believe, and obey. Thus, **obedience** is the cornerstone of application. Therefore, Prayer Warriors, my prayer is that the very character of prayer has made an indelible print on the manuscript of your soul and that prayer has become a new powerful force in your own prayer life. Amen!

"We show [demonstrate] what we know [have learned] when we act [apply] on the fact we have learned."

# Chapter 12
## Confession of Sin a Must

Prior to making an accurate application, there is the need first to learn and become aware of what is to be considered. For example, before one applies for a job, there must be the realization that the person needs a job. No one is going to seek work unless there is a heart-felt need for it. In like manner, if God is to hear our prayers and for there to be a joyful communion of fellowship and the spirit of worship with the holy, august God of both heaven and earth, then one of the first crucial truths to be learned and grasped significantly is the confession and forgiveness of sin. Prayers of the wicked are an abomination in His holy sight.

*"God cannot stand the prayers of anyone who disobeys his Law"* (Proverbs 28:9, CEV).

Thus, Prayer Warriors, if you are serious about prayer and desire more than anything else the gracious spirit of worship in God's divine presence, and to live daily with the assurance that God does (present tense) and will hear (future tense) and answer your prayers, then the practice of a sinful lifestyle has to go! The blood of Jesus Christ must cover it. As the Living Bible paraphrases Proverbs 28:9,

*"God doesn't listen to the prayers of men who flout the law."*

This word **flout** is to regard God's Word with contempt. To me, it implies the attempt to be Christian without a serious confession of sin before God. This sinful spirit is an abomination in God's sight. Jesus died to destroy the works, purpose, efforts, and strategies of the devil (read First John 3:8). For us to think that God will honor our prayer-efforts without a sincere, prayer of confession of sin to Him is the greatest degree of spiritual ignorance.

Luke, the apostle, writing about the apostles and the immeasurable power of the Holy Spirit, referred to Paul's message, declaring David as having been "a man after God's own heart" (Acts 13:22; see I Samuel 13:14). Yet David was to learn the grave lesson that unless there is confession and repentance of sin, there cannot be the closeness and union with Him, the everlasting God. Sin separates and creates a barrier between God and man (see Isaiah 59:1, 2). God does not and never will allow the joy of intimate fellowship with Him exist when sin is the predominant factor in one's life. David attempted to hide his sin of murder and adultery from God and remain a righteous, upright king. It was impossible, however. To have the joy of God's salvation in his heart and soul there was the demand of repentance and confession before his God. Psalm 51 records David's confession.

Verse one is David's prayer; his asking God for mercy. Sin is a direct denial of God, His power, and His holiness. David knew that he deserved God's judgment. He had deliberately sinned against the moral law of God. His only hope of forgiveness and deliverance was to surrender himself totally upon the sacrifice of God's love and mercy.

David recognized that forgiveness of any sin is the result of God's mercy. David's plea to God was:

*"Have mercy upon me, O God, according to Your lovingkindness."*

He was keenly aware that his being forgiven of his sin was not based on his prayer, even though prayer was essential. His forgiveness was based on the character of God, His MERCY! "For God's mercy to hold any meaning for us, we must first begin to understand the intensity of God's holiness and the immensity of man's sin. The depth of [God's] mercy is in direct relation to the gravity of the wrong."[1] David knew that he deserved no forgiveness, only God's judgment. His forgiveness would come only through the mercy of God's grace. God's mercy toward David and to us is simply an expression of His eternal LOVE. Thus David asked God to bathe him in the fresh stream of forgiveness *"according to the multitude of* [His] *tender mercies."*

David not only asked God to forgive him, but also to "blot out" his transgressions. Sin is a fighting, rebellious nature against God. This spiritual struggle, opposing God, was taking its toll on David. He could not bury his contemptible sin deep in his subconscious mind. In verse three he admits that his transgression is ever before him. There is no activity in which David could engage himself, even with all the responsibility of kingship, that would allow him to dismiss his horrible sin (and sin is horrible) from his mind. He was tormented daily for he says, *"And my sin is always before me"* (v. 3b). Wanting to be rid of the guilt of sin that had separated him from his God, he asked Him *"to blot out his transgression."*

Verse two records David's strong, sincere desire to be washed clean of the filth sin had created. He asked God "to wash" and "to cleanse" him thoroughly of his iniquity. Prayer Warriors, that is the power of Jesus' death and resurrection. The blood of Jesus Christ enables Him to become our Saviour. His blood through our confession and repentance washes us and cleanses us thoroughly and completely.

As David admitted his sin and acknowledged it before God, verse four reveals the very depth of the conflict. He says in an intense prayer-tone to the One he had overtly wearied, *"Against You, You only, have I sinned, And done this evil in Your sight"* (read First Samuel 12:13). David saw sin for what it truly is—**evil against God Himself!**

Prayer warriors, one of the most acknowledged facts we must remember every day is that satan is seeking ways and means to cause us to sin. Remember our sins are not toward satan; they are rebellion against God who sent His Son to die for our sins that we may be delivered and have victory over them. Praise the Lord that we can rejoice in the fact that there is victory, victorious power, conquering power over the evil that sin causes.

> *"For whatever is born of God overcomes the world. And this is the victory that overcomes the world—our faith. Who is he who overcomes the world, but he who believes that Jesus is the Son of God?"* (1 John 5:4-5)

David realized that confession to God was the means, the only means, to witness God's peace, washing, and cleansing of his soul. David states in Psalm 66:18 these words relative to confession:

> *"If I regard iniquity in my heart, the Lord will not hear."*

David recognized that prayer, no matter how diligent and enthusiastic the prayer-tone may be, if unforgiving sin is existing, then God has chosen not to hear the prayer, much less to answer. Listen to David's excited pitch as he hastens to add his confidence in prayer and God's response when sin has been forgiven.

> *"But certainly God has heard me; He has attended to the voice of my prayer"* (Psalm 66:19).

The heartbeat of this chapter is to make us acutely conscious that sin will rob us totally of any prayer effectiveness; and as active sin seeps into the Christian experience, it will steal the worshipful atmosphere which should be realized as one goes to the dynamic throne of God. Hence, Prayer Warriors, remember to be on guard and remember the role of satan to cause your prayer life to be polluted with the stink of sin. Read often Psalm 66:18 and then rejoice as you read and claim Psalm 66:19! Sin is not to have dominion over us. It is God and God only who is, and that relationship gives powerful meaning to our praying! Just think, Prayer Warriors, if David had gone to his "prayer closet" rather than going to the roof to gaze lustfully at a woman, that sinful blot would not have stained his life. The Apostle Paul is very definite as he alerts the Church in Rome of spiritual awareness:

> *"Do not let sin control your puny body any longer; do not give in to its sinful desires. Do not let any part of your bodies become tools of wickedness, to be used for sinning; but give yourselves completely to God—every part of you—for you are back from death and you want to be tools in the hands of God, to be used for his good purposes. Sin need never again be your master...* (Romans 6:12-14a, TLB).

The way to obtain spiritual victory over sin, the deceitful works of satan, after one's confession of sin, is to possess a spiritual hunger and seek definite directive from God through the power of the Holy Spirit each day. If you enter into the day trusting and depending on your own self, then you are a prime candidate to fall trap to satan's tactics. E. M. Bounds admonishes:

> "The men who have done the most for God in this world have been early on their knees. He who fritters away the early morning, its opportunity and freshness, in other pursuits than seeking God's will, makes poor headway seeking Him the rest of the day. He will be in the last place the remainder of the day."[2]

The Word of God and prayer to Him are the strong pillars that will fortify us against active sin. David said, *"Your word I have hidden in my heart, that I might not sin against You"* (Psalm 119:11).

David knew the secret of witnessing the grace of God and

experiencing forgiveness. It demanded *"a broken spirit, a broken and a contrite heart; these, O God, You will not despise"* (Psalm 51:17). Prayer Warriors that is still the necessary remedy: confession and forgiveness of sin. Don't allow sin to rob you of the victory and answer to prayer. God desires to answer, but He demands a life of holiness and consecration to Him!

## NOTES

[1] Mary Foxwell Loeks, *The Glorious Names of God*, "Merciful God," Baker Book House, Grand Rapids, MI. Copyright 1986, pp. 69.
[2] *The Complete Works of E. M. Bounds on Prayer*, "Begin the Day with Prayer", Copyright 1990 by Baker Book House Company, p. 464.

# Chapter 13
## *The Spiritual Position for Prayer*

To me, Prayer Warriors, chapters 13 and 14 are the most serious ones in this book, for they convict me of my own humble position I am to desire in my own personal "prayer life."

During a person's life here on earth, wouldn't it be interesting to determine how much time is devoted to simply **sitting**? It seems to me that this posture is one of the most favorite of all. An infant, for example, spends its first months either lying or sitting. Parents are thrilled when their baby begins sitting up straight and balancing itself in the upright position.

A family may travel for hours and cover hundreds of miles sitting in the car, bus, train, or airplane, and yet when they reach their destination and enter the home of friends or relatives, the first thing they want to do is sit. We don't enjoy standing while eating (at least I don't); I naturally look for a seat. While I was in the army, I bivouacked on numerous occasions. When eating, I always looked for a tree stump or whatever else I could find on which to place my canteen. I could never eat holding my army plate and cup in my hands or on my lap. It was much more comfortable if I could find a place for the food and to sit. Who wants to stand while eating, watching TV, or waiting to bowl? Much money is spent at sport events as spectators pay for "good seats" to watch and enjoy some sport. There are many more examples which could be shared to explain "sitting" as being man's favorite position, but the point of emphasis, I believe, has been made.

### THE POSITION OF ROYALTY AND AUTHORITY— SITTING!

Where a person sits may very well symbolize his influence and place among men. Saul, who was to become Israel's first king, is introduced to us as a young man exceedingly handsome, and head and shoulders above all others (see 1 Samuel 9:2). He appears to be a humble man in spirit and attitude. Not realizing that he, by the design of the Jehovah God, had been chosen to be the first king of Israel, Saul doesn't understand Samuel's statement when he says to

Saul:

> *And anyway, you own all the wealth of Israel now!* (1 Samuel 9:20b, TLB).

In fact, Saul informs Samuel that he is from the tribe of Benjamin, the smallest tribe, and that his family is not of important stock at all; meaning, his family doesn't have any influence of decision-making within the tribe of Benjamin. His conclusion is:

*"You* [Samuel] *must have the wrong man!"* (see 1 Samuel 9:22).

Saul does not become haughty or self-exalted as he hears Samuel's words of honor being placed upon him. Samuel has planned a special meal in Saul's honor and has invited thirty guests. Notice the importance of position. Samuel does not seat Saul in a place of insignificance; he places him and his servant, not in a corner, but *"had them sit in the place of honor among those who were invited"* (see 1 Samuel 9:22).

Wouldn't it be embarrassing to be sitting at a banquet table or at a wedding feast and to be requested to move so that an honored guest may be seated where you were sitting? For myself I would be so humiliated, I would want to exit myself as quickly as possible! Jesus Himself warned against sitting or seeking to grab a seat of honor without first being invited by the host (see Luke 14:7-11; Proverbs 25:6, 7). Jesus also makes it very clear that he who seeks to exalt himself before others will be humbled (see Luke 14:11).

Yes, where we sit oftentimes symbolizes royalty, recognition, and authority of kingship. Such was the case of Solomon, the son of King David. David had sat on the throne as king of Israel for forty years. It was he, not King Saul, who unified and fortified Israel. Through his military and ingenious skills, being led by the Spirit and direction of God Himself, Israel emerged a great, powerful nation. Now as David had advanced in years, it was time for someone else to assume the position of kingship. After much conflict and political turmoil, initiated by his son Adonijah who was attempting to declare himself the new king of Israel, David authorized Zadok the priest to anoint Solomon the next king of Israel. Notice again the word **sit** and its symbolism.

> *Also the king* [David] *said thus, "Blessed be the Lord God*

*of Israel, who has given one to sit on my throne this day, while my eyes see it"* (1 Kings 1:48).

## THE MOST SIGNIFICANT "SITTING" OF ALL

In my home I have a recliner; my favorite chair. There I relax when I read a book, drink coffee, or watch the news on TV. In the kitchen, I have a comfortable chair that enables me to enjoy a delicious meal. (I have just bought myself a new desk chair to sit on when using my computer; it is really comfortable.) Naturally there is more furniture in my house, but these three pieces, used for the purpose of sitting, are important commodities in my home. Their basic purpose is for my comfort; they provide physical ease. Notice, though, my sitting in them is not basically for spiritual growth or spiritual insight. This type of sitting has nothing to do with my eternal destiny, only my own physical enjoyment.

In like manner, one may be able to boast of sitting in the chair of authority, influence, or prestige, that of being able to make demands on others, and even cause them to shudder because of one's presence or authority. Your position may enable you to stand head and shoulders above all others. Yet one's political, economic or prestigious position in this earthly existence does not and will not prepare one for eternity. No earthly "sitting" is the most important of all!

## *DAVID HOLY, SPIRITUAL SITTING*

Prayer Warriors, let David challenge you to a deeper understanding of the meaning of a "spiritual position" before God Himself. David had been a forceful king and a military genius, defeating all his enemies, *"and the Lord had given him rest from all the enemies all around"* (see 2 Samuel 7:1). Thus, as David's mind was at rest and set free of military planning, he thought of the comfortable, elaborate house which he had and of the ark of God simply dwelling inside tent curtains. In reverence to his God, he desired to build a permanent temple to house the ark of God. However, Nathan the prophet had a vision from God, which he shared with David. The heart of the message to David was that he was not to be the one to build this temple; his son Solomon was the chosen one (see 2 Samuel 7: 2-17). How does David respond to this change of plans?

> *Then King David went in and **sat** [emphasis mine] before the Lord . . .* (2 Samuel 7:18).

Verse eighteen tells me that David desired to spend some serious moments with his Jehovah God. This was no rushing, twinkling, jiffy incident; David wanted to spend considerable time with his Lord. It was a time of **prayer!** (see 2 Samuel 7: 19-29). David sat on the earthly throne as king of Israel, but I do not believe that royal position is what made him great in the eyes of his Lord. His appetite for communion, fellowship, guidance of his God, and his determination to spend significant time in God's presence is, to me, what made David great, and a man after God's own heart. **David was a man of prayer; he sat before his Lord!**

After David had been anointed king of Israel, he captured Jerusalem and defeated the Jebusites who lived there. He then took up residence in Jerusalem and named the city, the City of David (see 2 Samuel 5:6-9). The power of his strength, though, was not his self-ability; verse ten discloses his source of strength: *"And he became more and more powerful, because the Lord God Almighty was with him"* (NIV).

Oh! Prayer Warriors, for us, through the eye of **faith**, to understand God as David did. As God Almighty was with David, He has promised to be with us also. Later when the Philistines learned that David had been anointed king of Israel, they went searching for him with a full force of military strength. When David was made aware of the Philistines and their opposition, what did he do? Immediately he went to his stronghold (fortress) which became his "prayer closet" and he sought God's direction:

> *So David inquired of the Lord, saying, "Shall I go up against the Philistines? Will You deliver them into my hands?" And the Lord said to David, "Go up, for I will doubtless deliver the Philistines into your hand"* (2 Samuel 5:19).

---

**When God is with a person, defeat will be the results to the enemy!**

---

David wants to know precisely God's will against the enemy.

Prayer Warriors, that means much time must be spent with Him to get the answer. If you want to know God's will, then sit, without getting in a hurry, and allow God to speak to you. The only way David could receive the right answer was to sit before his Lord and listen to His directions.

David was mindful that it was not up to himself to determine the strategy against the enemy; through prayer God would reveal effective plans and strategies against them. Evidently the Philistines had not grasped the fact that when God is with a person, defeat will be the results. Once again they went up against David. His response again is an eye opener to us when faced with the challenge of decision. David doesn't conclude that because he had crushed the Philistines in the previous battle that he could be totally confident of victory once again. (Prayer Warriors, notice David's confidence is not in himself, but in his God.) He sought the will, the leadership, the instruction from his Lord; and God was very specific to David as how the enemy was to be crushed.

> "Therefore David inquired of the Lord, and He said, "You shall not go up; circle around behind them, and come upon them in front of the mulberry trees. And it shall be, when you hear the sound of marching in the tops of the mulberry trees, then you shall advance quickly. For then the Lord will go out before you to strike the camp of the Philistines" (2 Samuel 5:23, 24).

Observe the 1, 2, 3 steps of David. **One,** he is faced with a challenge against the Philistines, David **goes directly** to his Lord, **sits** before Him and **prays.** Praying is an indispensable aspect of the Christian life. **Next,** the Lord gives David **specific directions** as how to face the challenge. Getting explicit instructions and directions from our King and Master are essential. The **third step,** to me, is the climax for it tells us how he reacted to God's instructions to him. Verse 25, "And David did so, as the Lord, commanded him; and he drove back the Philistines from Geba as far as Gezer."

David did not neglect this **third step,** which is **obedience.** "And David did so, as the Lord commanded him." Obedience, Prayer Warriors, **OBEDIENCE!** That is the power within the Christian experience! As David prayed and God answered, He didn't question God, but he simply went forth and did it, and he witnessed victory over the Philistines!

David had had experiences of trusting His Jehovah God! I believe his middle name may have been "Trust God"! When he faced both the lion and bear, he defeated them not through his own physical strength but through his faith and trust in the Lord. Later he overthrew and defeated the mighty Philistine Goliath (see 1 Samuel 17:34, 35).

Oh! God, awaken our hearts, not only to pray, but also to obedience to Your will! David's desire was to sit before his Lord and listen to Him. As I read the Psalms, which, to me, is the "Prayer Book" of the Bible, I am convinced that David found being before His God in prayer, listening to Him, and then being obedient taught him precious insight of God's will more than any thing else. He said the following to his Lord:

*"Give heed to the voice of my cry, my king and my God, for to You I will pray. My voice You shall hear in the morning, O Lord; in the morning I will direct to You, and I will look up"* (Psalm 5:2, 3).

---

### *How often will YOU sit before the Eternal King?*

---

David was mindful that it was not up to him to determine the strategy against the enemy; through prayer God would reveal effective plans and strategies against them.

Isn't it fascinating to read of God's workings and the unorthodox methods He uses? No wonder the Scripture says that God's ways and thoughts are beyond our little finite minds (see Isa. 55:8, 9). Enthusiastically, David showers praise upon his Lord. He reflects how God has led him and the victories God has given him. Thus when he considers building a permanent temple for his Lord, he simply enters his "prayer closet" to spend time in God's holy presence, and **sits** before his Lord, and declares:

*. . . This was a small thing in Your sight! O Lord God* (2 Samuel 7:19).

David sees responsibilities and even life itself through God's perspective. He recognizes a fact that all of us need to grasp and understand.

As he has reflected how God had given him victory after victory, he comes to the conclusion that all these victories are a "small thing" in God's sight. That is, it is God who is the All-powerful and the Unlimited One!

When we, the Church wakens to this spiritual revelation, then it will move and influence the world for Jesus Christ; for it will then, like David, inquire of the Lord rather than trusting in its own "Christian humanism," that is, attempting to do the Lord's work trusting in its own strength to accomplish God's purpose. David's "spiritual position" was his sitting before his Lord and King.

Psalm 89:20 relates the gracious honor God had placed on David:

> "I [God] have found My servant David; with My holy oil
> I have anointed him, with whom My hand shall be established;
> also My arm shall strengthen him."

My personal opinion is that God declares David a man after His own heart because he was a man of prayer. He desired **to sit** before his Jehovah God and worship and praise Him through prayer! When the Church really hungers and thirsts for "the anointing oil" of God's power through the ministry of the Holy Spirit then it will have faith to move mountains, mountains of opposition!

## MARY'S FAVORITE POSITION—
## SITTING BEFORE HER LORD

Mary, Martha, and Lazarus! What a trio! What a family. Their home was in Bethany, just a few miles from Jerusalem. What a family to have in your own home town as your next door neighbor. I believe their home was one of Jesus' favorite places. Of course, the Garden of Gethsemane was His favorite, for it was His "prayer closet," His altar place to spend much time with His heavenly Father. The home of that gracious trio was where Jesus could relax, not face opposition, and not have to defend his relationship of being God's Son. They loved Jesus, respected Him, and enjoyed having Him in their home. Of the three, though, Mary, to me, is the one who stands out. Her character of **humility** is so obvious as one reflects on the few Scriptures that mention her. Notice she is never seen standing upright before Jesus. Every reference of her portrays her at the feet of Jesus. Here, it appears, is where she feels she belongs and even longs to be.

> "*And she [Martha] had a sister called Mary, who also sat at Jesus' feet and heard His word*" (Luke 10:39).

What a position of worship! Mary had only one craving—**to listen and hear what Jesus had to say!** Oh, how Martha was missing the gracious opportunity she had. She had invited Jesus into her house (see Luke 10:38), yet she was not sensitive to the opportunity. Her mind was on feeding Jesus; Mary saw an opportunity for Jesus to feed her. She simply sat at Jesus' feet and waited for Him to declare His word to her. Martha even became distracted and frustrated, working and planning the meal. "Why doesn't my sister come into the kitchen and assist me?" She even grumbled to Jesus of her sister's attitude. Martha certainly didn't anticipate Jesus' mild rebuke to her.

**Martha wants to entertain Jesus; have Him to sit at her table. Mary wants to worship Jesus and** *sit at His feet* **and be fed spiritually!**

> "*And Jesus answered and said to her, "Martha, Martha, you are worried and troubled about many things. But one thing is needed, and Mary has chosen that good part, which will not be taken away from her*" (Luke 10:41, 42)

---

*Martha's interest was to ENTERTAIN Jesus;*
*Mary desired simply to WORSHIP Jesus!*

---

We don't learn God's will for our lives or for the Church by telling God what we want to do or going to do and then asking Him to bless our own predetermined plans. If our minds are already made up then God cannot and will not direct us. We learn by "sitting at the feet of Jesus" as Mary did and allowing Him to teach us. Oh, to be quiet, to stop talking, and allow the Holy Spirit to speak and direct our hearts. All Mary wanted to do was sit before Jesus and enjoy and witness His presence. Jesus even told Martha that Mary had chosen the "good part" and she wouldn't lose it.

Prayer Warriors, **reading** the Word of God and **listening** to the prompting of the Holy Spirit are the keys that unlock the doors of obedience and God's guidance. Mary Geegh, who was a missionary to India for thirty-eight years, said in her small book titled *God Guides*: "I determine to listen to God for guidance in all matters, and I promised Him I would obey whatever He told me." [1]

John, the apostle, in chapter 12 records Jesus going to the trio's house six days before the Passover in Jerusalem. Once again we see Martha preparing the meal and being concerned about serving. Lazarus, whom Jesus had raised from the grave, was sitting at the table with Him. What is Mary doing? Verse 3 explains:

> "Then Mary took a pound of very costly oil of spike nard, anointed the feet of Jesus, and wiped His feet with her hair. And the house was filled with the fragrance of the oil."

As you read this passage, Prayer Warriors, don't you see, feel, and realize how much we have failed and are failing in the attitude and spirit of worshiping the Trinity? Mary's whole disposition is clothed in the garment of humility. When she sees Jesus, neither food, social activities, nor anything else occupies her mind. She sees only Jesus! She is absorbed with only one thought: "sitting at the feet of Jesus"! Martha, Lazarus, and the apostles are there in her home. She sees none of them, only Jesus! She anoints His feet, wipes them with her hair, "*And the house was filled with the fragrance of the oil*" (v. 3).

Oh how the Church of Jesus Christ needs an earth-shaking experience with the Master of our souls. Do we know how to sit and patiently wait for God's revelation to us? Oh, for our hearts and our worship at Church to be filled with the holy oil of His presence! Mary had the insight of genuine worship, **sitting at the feet of Jesus!**

There is one more scene of Mary that I want to share with you. Mary and Martha are heart-broken. Their brother Lazarus is dying; in desperation they sent word to Jesus. They were confident that Jesus some way or other would be able to sustain the life of their brother. However, Jesus delays His going to Mary and Martha. When Jesus does arrive, Martha is the first one to meet Him. Later Mary went to Jesus and when she came to Him "*she fell down at His feet, saying to Him, Lord, if You had been here, my brother would not have died*" (John 11:32).

Jesus did perform the miracle of healing and Lazarus was raised from the dead. That is not my main emphasis, though. Once again,

Mary is seen at the **feet of Jesus!** Even though her brother has died and she seems to imply that Jesus may have failed her for His not coming to them sooner, she still is full of reverence for Jesus. She can't stand upright and talk to Jesus even though the subject is of her dead brother. His feet, the feet of Jesus! There is where Mary seems to belong!

What is special about Mary? She is never seen following Jesus during His ministry. She certainly doesn't appear to possess any special talents or gifts. Certainly, she wasn't concerned about providing a good meal for Jesus or entering into an exciting conversation with Him. There are basically only these four scenes of the life of Mary portrayed in the Scriptures. Yet, to me, Mary is a very special person and Jesus had many communions with her. Why? Because Jesus could say *"Mary has chosen the good part, which will not be taken away from her"* (Luke 10:42).

Yes, Prayer Warriors, if you want to know God's will for you, *sit at His feet.* If you want guidance for your daily life, sit at His feet. If you want physical and spiritual strength for the day, sit at Jesus' feet. If you have a problem of fear facing you as you enter into a new day, then start the day sitting at His feet. In fact, if you have no problems, no difficulties, no heartaches, everything in your life appears to be totally secured and there are no hindrances at all, still start the day sitting at the feet of Jesus and worship and praise Him for all the blessings you are enjoying. Yes, to me, Mary is very special in the Word of God for she is always seen sitting at Jesus' feet. (Let prayer be your key for the day and your lock of the night.)

"Doing" is an important aspect of the Christian life, but, Prayer Warriors, if you are really serious about God's will in your life, you will learn much more by waiting and listening! That means time devoted to the "prayer closet," spending time in God's holy presence and allowing Him to tell you the plans He has for you. Then you are in the position to do the "DOING"! It would be well if we Christians would follow the instructions given to little Samuel by the priest Eli.

> *"Go and lie down again, and if he calls again, say, 'Yes, Lord, I'm listening.'"* So Samuel went back to bed, And the Lord came and called as before, *"Samuel! Samuel!"* And Samuel replied, *"Yes, I'm listening."* (1 Samuel 3: 8b-10, TLB).

Both David and Mary sat before the Lord; little Samuel had a listening ear to the voice of the Lord. Prayer Warriors, that is the secret of victory—**LEARN TO LISTEN!**

I am convinced that one of the greatest needs for us Christians and the Christian Church is that of learning what it means to wait before God and sit at His feet and learn!

### WHERE ARE YOU SITTING?

The issue is not whether you are sitting or not; we all sit. The vital point is where! We ourselves have chosen where we will "sit." Let Psalm 107:10, 11 (AMP) speak to your heart as you read:

> *"Some sat* [sit] *in darkness and in the shadow of death, being bound in affliction and in irons, Because they rebelled against the word of God, and spurned the counsel of the Most High."*

Do you get it? Really get it? Spiritually, many people are sitting in darkness. They have chosen to be bound in the chains of affliction and the pit of sin itself. Why? Because they have rebelled, fought against, and have deliberately rejected the Word of the Lord. They have spurned the counsel, the wooing of the Holy Spirit. Is that where you are now sitting as you read this chapter? Or are you like David and Mary; that is, possessing a desire to sit at Jesus' feet and worship Him? Do you have a "listening ear" as little Samuel had?

> *Sitting at the feet of Jesus,*
> *Where can mortal be more blessed?*
> *There I lay my sins and sorrows*
> *And, when weary, find sweet rest.*
> *Sitting at the feet of Jesus,*
> *There I love to weep and pray,*
> *While I from His fullness gather*
> *Grace and comfort every day.*

### NOTES

[1]Mary Geegh, *God Guides*, Pray America, P.O. Box 14070, Lansing, Mi. 48901-4070, 12th printing, 1995, p. 2.

# Chapter 14
## *I Can NOW Pray! HALLELUJAH!*

> *Or do you think that I cannot now pray to My Father, and He will provide Me with more than twelve legions of angels?* (Matthew 26:53).

### THE SIGNIFICANCE OF A ONE-SYLLABLE THREE-LETTER WORD

There is a little three-letter word that has only one vowel. Yet it is such an integral part of our vocabulary. No doubt, if we kept a record as to how many times this little one-syllable three-letter word is used in our own vocabulary within any one 24-hour period, we would be amazed. We use it constantly without much forethought of its meaning or significance. Yet this little word has such a powerful meaning that it is used countless times in Scripture. The word is **"NOW."**

The meaning of this word emphasizes time as being "at the moment" or "immediate." It has nothing to do with the past or future. There is absolutely no waiting; there is a readiness for action, to complete, to accomplish the task at the present moment. The King James Version first uses the word **"now"** in the words of Adam:

> *And Adam said: This is* **now** *[emphasis mine] bone of my bones, and flesh of my flesh; she shall be called Woman, because she was taken out of Man"* (Gen. 2:23).

Adam, who had been put into a deep sleep by the Lord so that Eve could be made from his rib by the power of God, looked at her, saw her completeness and said, "This is the proper time, the right time; she is ready at this precise moment to be named." As he saw her body formed by God into a perfect specimen, he could proclaim her being "**now** bone of my bone and flesh of my flesh." Thus, there was no more waiting and Adam named her "Woman," because she was taken out of man.

How many times have we waited for the definite moment to act? For example, we may be at an exit sign, stop sign, or stoplight either driving a car or simply walking and having to wait to determine the "right time, the right moment" to drive or walk. If someone else is accompanying us, we may ask if it is safe. "Can we go now?" we may inquire, meaning, is this the right time, the proper time, the "safe time" to move from our present position? Adam thought to himself, "I don't need to wait any longer; she is ready to be named," so he acted, named her "Woman."

Genesis 18: 20, 21 (AMP) has reference to God's immediate action. Verse 20 records what had come to God's ears as to the conduct and lifestyle of Sodom and Gomorrah.

> *And the Lord said, Because the shriek [of the sins] of Sodom and Gomorrah is great, and their sin is exceedingly grievous; I will go down **now** [emphasis mine], and see whether they have done altogether [as vilely and wickedly] as is the cry of it, which is come to Me; and if not, I will know.*

The wickedness of Sodom and Gomorrah penetrated the ears of God. Thus, He declared the time had come to see for Himself the depth of their sin.

The scene is the wickedness of two cities. Who is paying any attention to them? Is anyone taking notice? Rest assure God knows the sin, every sin, in the heart of man. God misses absolutely nothing. He Himself waits just so long and then He moves into action. The **NOW**! The moment of decision becomes a reality with God.

*Then the Lord rained brimstone and fire on Sodom and Gomorrah, from the Lord out of the heavens* (Gen. 18:24).

We serve God Jehovah who is Almighty, All-loving, and All-merciful; but He is also a God who acts in each **now** situation! He sees! He knows! He evaluates! and then the **now** becomes a fact, and God moves into action!

Gen. 6: 5, 6, 7 (TLB) records God's move into the **"now"** action.

> *When the Lord God saw the extent of human wickedness, and that the trend and direction of men's lives were only towards evil, he was sorry he had made them. It broke his heart. And he said, "I will blot out from the face of the earth all mankind that I created. Yes, and the animals too, and the reptiles and the birds. For I am sorry that I made them."*

God had taken a serious look at the lifestyle of these two wicked cities, Sodom and Gomorrah. Their sin had become a sounding ring in His ear and a foul odor to His nostrils. God states: "I will go down now and see…" The verb phrase "will go" indicates God's determination. There is no longer any waiting; God is going to see at this moment the wickedness and sin that have absorbed these two cities. If it had not been for the righteousness of Noah, God would have destroyed the whole earth and every thing within it. All would have become ETERNITY once again.

Sin makes a person, a city, a nation evil in God's holy sight. If sin creeps into the lifestyle of the Church, oh, how that must grieve the heart of God! From what God observed He declared the time had come to destroy these two cities. There was no righteous Noah in the city, only the wickedness of sinful men and women. Fire and brimstone were poured out upon them. The destruction was complete! Nothing was left!

## DON'T WAIT! PRAY NOW!

By **now** (used intentionally) you may be saying that is interesting Bible history, but what does the destruction of Sodom and Gomorrah have to do with prayer? It doesn't except for the fact that God Himself considered **NOW** an important occasion for His time of decision-making.

A few years ago I was reading in Matthew chapter 26 during my morning devotions. As I was prayerfully reading and meditating, I pictured Jesus there in the Garden of Gethsemane. He had poured out His heart and soul before His heavenly Father, seeking His Father's will and proclaiming *"not as I will, but as You will"* (Matthew 26:39b). At the close of His prayerful agony, the enemy came on the scene. Judas, by a betrayal kiss, identified Jesus as the One the soldiers were to capture and take to trial. Then one of His disciples (possibly Peter), thinking he was coming to Jesus' rescue, *"stretched out his hand and drew his sword, struck the servant of the high priest, and cut off his ear"* (Matthew 26: 51b).

I was in deep spiritual thought and communion with the Father as I continued my devotional reading. When I read verse 53, all heaven opened up to me. I saw! I grasped! I understood!—ever so clearly that Jesus was not and had never been a victim. Listen to your heart, grasp, and cling to these powerful words uttered by Jesus Christ to the one who had drawn his sword to deliver Jesus from His vicious enemies:

> *Or do you think that I cannot* **NOW** *[emphasis mine] pray to My Father, and He will provide Me with more than twelve legions of angels?* (Matthew 26:53).

Prayer Warriors, I read that verse and stopped reading. My heart was pounding; my eyes burst forth with joyful tears. This forceful, potent thought hit the bull's eye of my heart and soul. Jesus had notified His disciple what He could have done right then if He so wanted. Even as the mob bounced upon Him, He could have prayed right then to His Father. As Judas was planting his deceiving lips on Jesus' cheek, Jesus could have right then whispered a prayer to His Father and thousands of military angels would have surrounded the enemy. He was not a helpless casualty to the angry mob. All He had to do right then (I continue to use "right then"), at that precise moment, that very instant, was **pray!** and all heaven would have come on the scene. The Garden of Gethsemane would have become the battleground surrounded with the military angel soldiers of heaven. That, Prayer Warriors, is how Jesus could have exercised His power!

However, Jesus chose not to seek His Father's rescuing power. He chose to remain submissive to His Father's will and **die** for you and me.

After remaining silent for some time, feeding on the revelation of the power of God and the victory available to me, I saw the implication of that little three-letter, one-syllable word **now!** I broke forth in prayerful utterance to the Lord. I saw the instance of prayer. I said to myself, "I **now** can pray for my wife," and I prayed for her. "I **now** can pray for my pastor and Church," I said; "I can **now** pray for missionary families," and I did. I broke forth with musical tone of prayer. I prayed for those blessed Pioneer Crusaders of EHC who are scattered throughout the world delivering gospel tracts to every home. Ever since I committed myself to faithful, daily prayer, I have known that I can always pray. One does not have to wait until things, situations, or conditions are just right to pray. It is just that the Holy Spirit drove the thought of the **NOW** of prayer into the depth of my soul. It was such a dynamic, spiritual experience for me.

For more than an hour I simply sat at the feet of Jesus and

uttered the word **NOW** to my heavenly Father and prayed for whatever or whomever God through the Holy Spirit placed on my mind. Again, this spiritual fact I had known for years was revived deeply in my soul and became alive bubbling up in my heart.

Prayer Warriors, we never have to wait for any particular moment in time to pray. There is always the **NOW** when it comes to prayer! Jesus, said (paraphrase), "Disciple, aren't you aware, don't you know what I can do right now if I so desire? I can call the total host of military angels to come down from heaven, destroy My enemies, and claim complete victory!"

Prayer Warriors, be now encouraged; don't become a victim of any circumstance in which you find yourself. Jesus chose not to pray the prayer of deliverance to His Father, but He could have, and God would have sent the soldiers of angels to rescue Him. The thought I want to leave with you in this book of prayer is we can **now** pray. No situation that we may be in has the power to stop our prayers. All we have to do is **PRAY!** God's power, His Son Jesus Christ, and the Holy Spirit are listening to us when we decide to talk to Them. In short, all that is within the name **Trinity** is waiting for us—the Church, His Prayer Warriors—to pray! **Serious-minded Prayer Warriors are those who pray! NOW you can pray! Are you praying??**

Many years ago my mother was crippled from the results of arthritis. She was confined the latter part of her life to the bed or wheel chair. I stopped by to see her on a Saturday morning. She said, "Son, I have much to pray about for tomorrow." I said, "You do!" Then she said, "You are preaching tomorrow, Dad [her husband] is preaching tomorrow, and Fred [my brother] is singing." Even though my mother was in physical pain, yet her thoughts were centered on her family: that of praying for us! She knew she need not wait but could right then enter into prayer to her Master for her family. Prayer Warriors, that is the blessing of prayer. We need not wait; we can pray NOW!

**Prayer Warriors, may God's Presence be showered upon you as you go to His heavenly Throne Daily!!**

Remember, victory doesn't come simply because you can pray; victory comes because you do **now** pray! Prayer Warriors, may we pray, continue to pray, and never fail to pray!

Prayer Warriors, I encourage you to equip yourselves with the following: First, establish a definite "prayer time" for each day; secondly, select a definite place to be your "Prayer Closet"; thirdly, read God's Word; let Him speak to you before you begin conversation with Him; fourthly, have a "Prayer Diary." That is, have some kind of notebook. When you are given "Prayer Requests" or there are definite "Lost People" for whom you are praying, write down these prayer requests, names and spiritual needs. Record the date of the prayer. That takes a few minutes, but looking at it will enable you to remember those for whom you are to pray. Surely, you don't want to say you will pray for someone and then forget to do so. I believe that grieves the Holy Spirit. For my wife and me, having the prayer needs written in our "spiritual Prayer Diary" enables us to recall the need for prayer. Also, as God answers our prayer, we put down the date of the answering; and we together praise Him for hearing and answering.

*Keep on* **[NOW]** *[my emphasis] praying* (1 Thessalonians 5:17, NLT).

*But the end of all things is at hand; therefore be serious and watchful in your prayers"* (1 Peter 4:7).

*The end of the world is coming soon. Therefore, be earnest and disciplined in your prayers* (1 Peter 4:7, NLT)

## *About the Author*

Dr. Leroy Jolly is a man whose passion for intercessory prayer challenges others to become more serious about hearing from God. Dr. Jolly has an AB and BS degree from Oakland City University, Oakland City, Indiana. He was also honored with his Doctor of Divinity from there.

Dr. Jolly has pastored Churches in Indiana and Michigan. He has also taught high school English in both of those states.

Since 1989 Dr. Jolly have been leading, "Prayer Enrichment Revivals," throughout the United States. Through their efforts, well over a thousand people have committed themselves to be faith Prayer Warriors.

For more information or to book Dr. Jolly for speaking engagements, or radio and television interviews contact:

PRAYER ENRICHMENT REVIVALS
120 W. Suffolk Court
Flint, MI 48507

Email: leroyjolly@comcast.net
Phone: (810) 603-2518

# Book Order Form

## PRAYER WARRIORS:
## Serious Minded Pray-ers

Name _____
Address _____
City _____ State _____ Zip _____
Phone _____ Fax _____
Email _____

| | |
|---|---|
| Quantity | |
| Price *(each)* | $10.95 |
| Subtotal | |
| S & H *(each)* | $2.99 |
| MI Tax 6% | |
| *TOTAL* | |

METHOD OF PAYMENT:

❏ Check or Money Order (*Make payable to*: PriorityONE Publications)

❏ Visa   ❏ Master Card   ❏ American Express

Acct No. _____

Expiration Date (*mmyy*) _____ CVV _____

Signature _____

*Mail your payment with this form to:*
PriorityONE Publications
P. O. Box 725
Farmington, MI 48332
(800) 596-4490 – Toll Free
URL: http://www.p1pubs.com
Email: info@p1pubs.com

www.ingramcontent.com/pod-product-compliance
Lightning Source LLC
Chambersburg PA
CBHW031256290426
44109CB00012B/604